THE
LITTLE GIANT® BOOK
OF MATH PUZZLES

DERRICK NIEDERMAN

Sterling Publishing Co., Inc.
New York

To Eliza, Marlowe, and
all the bright young kids at
North Yarmouth Memorial School

Illustrations by Jeff Sinclair

Library of Congress Cataloging-in-Publication Data

10   9   8   7   6   5   4   3   2   1

Published by Sterling Publishing Company, Inc.
387 Park Avenue South, New York, N.Y. 10016
© 2000 by Derrick Niederman
Distributed in Canada by Sterling Publishing
^{c}/o Canadian Manda Group, One Atlantic Avenue, Suite 105
Toronto, Ontario, Canada M6K 3E7
Distributed in Great Britain and Europe by Chris Lloyd
463 Ashley Road, Parkstone, Poole, Dorset, BH14 0AX, England
Distributed in Australia by Capricorn Link (Australia) Pty Ltd.
P.O.Box 6651. Baulkham Hillls, Business Centre, NSW 2153,
Australia

Sterling ISBN 0-8069-6565-7

Contents

How to Use This Book

This fat little book is packed with math puzzles of every type you can imagine—puzzles with numbers, puzzles with shapes, logic puzzles, trick puzzles, and a whole lot more. Some of the puzzles are fairly easy, but others are quite challenging. Which are which? Well, the difficulty level isn't the same for every solver out there, but to give you an idea of what to expect, we've placed pictures of our puzzle dog on each and every puzzle page, according to the following scale:

Difficulty Scale

You might not need a hint for this one.

A little tougher. Read it carefully!

You probably want to check the hints section

The toughest of the lot.
Bring family and friends together for these!

The Hints Section

All puzzles in this book have hints, whether you need them or not. You'll find the hints section between the puzzles and the answers. Remember, using a hint is perfectly okay if a particular puzzle stumps you. Sometimes the hints help you understand precisely what the question is asking, and other times they lead you on the way to the answer.

The Answer Section

One last thought. If a few of these puzzles escape you, don't get discouraged: You're not supposed to get every one of them the first time around. Many are devised to introduce you to brand new ways of thinking, approaches that you may not have seen before. I've tried to give you enough information in the Answers section so that the next time you come across this kind of puzzle, you'll think it's a piece of cake. So plug along. By the time you've finished this book—or even before—you will be thinking like a real puzzle solver.

Are you ready to get started? Have fun!

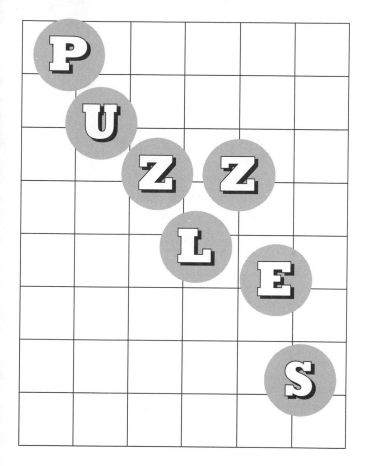

1 Easier by the Dozen

Place the numbers from 1 to 12 as follows:

The odd numbers go in the triangle. The even numbers go in the circle. The numbers that are divisible by three go in the square.

How will this look?

Hint on page 237.
Answer on page 280.

8

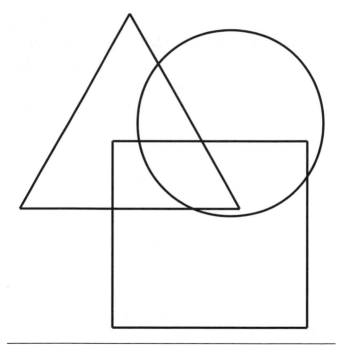

9

2 Waiting in Line

At the local sandwich shop, every customer who enters is given a number. On one particularly busy lunch hour, customers 17 through 31 were waiting to be called.

If you counted up all the waiting customers, how many would there be?

Hint on page 237.
Answer on page 280.

The numbers 1 through 9 are arranged in a circle. Can you divide the numbers into three groups—not changing the order—so that the sum of the numbers in each group is the same?

Hint on page 237.
Answer on page 281.

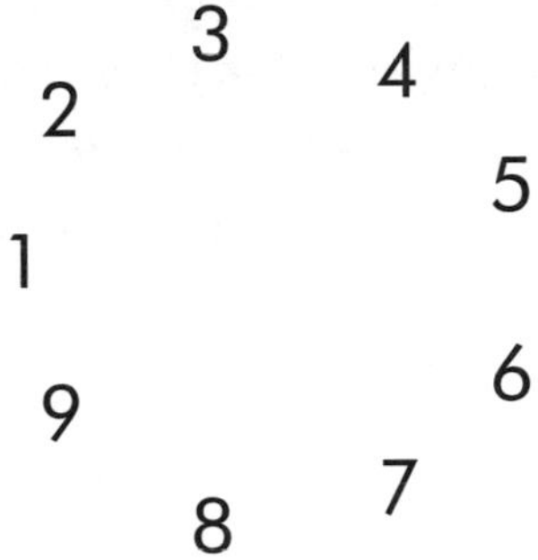

3

4

2

5

1

9

6

8

7

4 Who Is Faster?

Hector can run from the train station to his parents' house in eight minutes. His younger brother Darius can run the same distance eight times in one hour. (Not that he'd need to!) Who is faster?

Hint on page 237.
Answer on page 281.

Eggs-actly

If it takes three and a half minutes to boil an egg, how long does it take to boil four eggs? Be careful!

Hint on page 238.
Answer on page 282.

The Average Student

6

Melissa got a poor grade on her very first homework assignment at her new school—only one star out of a possible five stars! She was determined to do better. How many five-star ratings must she receive before she has an *average* rating of four stars?

Hint on page 238.
Answer on page 282.

7 **Just Checking**

Five kids sit down to play some games of checkers. If each one of the five kids plays one game with each of the others, what is the total number of games played?

Hint on page 238.
Answer on page 283.

20

8 Big Difference

Your challenge is to place the digits 2, 4, 6, and 7 into the boxes so that the difference between the two two-digit numbers is as big as possible.

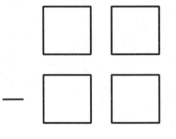

Hint on page 239.
Answer on page 284.

9 Not Such a Big Difference

What if you wanted to make the difference as *small* as possible?

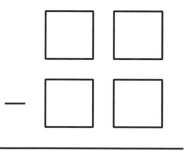

Hint on page 239.
Answer on page 284.

10 The One and Only

Believe it or not, there is only one number whose letters are in alphabetical order. Can you find it?

Hint on page 239.
Answer on page 284.

24

Letter Perfect

Rearrange the letters in the phrase ELEVEN PLUS TWO to create a new phrase with the same meaning!

Hint on page 239.
Answer on page 285.

How many rectangles can you find in this diagram?

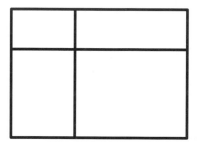

Hint on page 240.
Answer on page 285.

13 **Short Division**

See if you can perform the following division problem—without writing below the line!

$$7\,\overline{\smash{\big)}\,497{,}637{,}357}$$

Hint on page 240.
Answer on page 285.

14 Square Route

Four dots are arranged in a square. Starting at the upper left dot, draw three straight lines, each line going through one or more dots, so that you end up where you started. Every dot should have a line going through it.

●　　　●

●　　　●

Hint on page 240.
Answer on page 286.

15 The Missing Six

Place the six numbers below into the empty circles so that both sentences are true. Use each number once and only once.

①　②　③　④　⑤　⑦

◯ + ◯ = ◯

◯ − ◯ = ◯

Hint on page 240.
Answer on page 286.

16 No Honor among Theives

A valuable jewel was stolen from the Emerald City of Oz. Naturally, suspicion was placed on the three non-human visitors—the Scarecrow, the Tin Man, and the Cowardly Lion. They went to trial in front of the famous Wizard of Oz.

At their trial, the Scarecrow claimed that the Tin Man was innocent. The Tin Man claimed that the Cowardly Lion was innocent. As for the Cowardly Lion, he mumbled something that no one could understand.

Hint on page 241.
Answer on page 287.

30

If an innocent person never lies and a thief always lies, which if any of the three suspects is guilty?

17 Circular Reasoning

Only one of the four lines in the diagram on the next page divides the circle into two equal parts. Can you find that line?

Hint on page 241.
Answer on page 288.

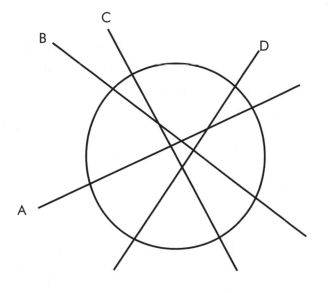

18　Trick or Treat

Halloween night was almost over, and fewer than 20 candies remained at the Greensleeve household. When the doorbell rang, Mr. Greensleeve figured it was the final group of trick-or-treaters for the night, so he figured he'd give away the rest of his candy.

At the door were two kids, one dressed as a ghost and the other as a lion. Mr. Greensleeve wanted to give them the same number of candies, but he noticed that when he

Hint on page 241.
Answer on page 288.

split the candies up, there was one left over.

At that point he noticed that a witch was hiding behind the lion. Now there were three trick-or-treaters. He tried dividing the candies equally among the three, but, again, one candy was left over.

Finally, Dracula jumped out from behind the ghost. Mr. Greensleeve tried dividing the candies among the *four* trick-or-treaters, but again there was one left over.

How many candies did Mr. Greensleeve have left when the doorbell rang?

19 Donut Try This at Home

Suppose a low-calorie donut has 95 percent fewer calories than a regular donut. How many low-calorie donuts would you need to eat to take in as many calories as you'd get from a regular donut?

Hint on page 242.
Answer on page 288.

20 The Long Way Around

If the height of the diagram on the next page is 8 units, and the length is 15 units, how far is it around the entire diagram?

Hint on page 242.
Answer on page 289.

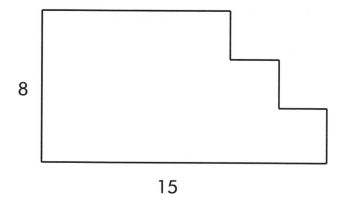

21 Connect the Dots

Can you place ten dots on a page using just five lines of four dots apiece?

Hint on page 242.
Answer on page 289.

22   **Pickup Sticks**

If you count out the matchsticks below, you'll see that the statement works out just fine. But can you rearrange the matchsticks so that the statement is still true and you don't need to do any counting?

||||||||||||||||||||||||||||| =29

Hint on page 242.
Answer on page 290.

23 Starting to Waffle

A portable waffle machine makes 120 waffles per minute. A stationary waffle machine makes 3 waffles per second. How many portable machines would you need if you wanted to equal the output of 4 stationary machines?

Hint on page 243.
Answer on page 290.

PLOP!

24 A Very Good Year

The year 1978 has an unusual property: When you add the 19 to the 78, you get 97—the middle two digits of the year!

What will be the next year to have this same property?

Hint on page 243.
Answer on page 290.

44

Professor Mathman went to the blackboard and demonstrated to his astonished class that one-half of eight was equal to three! What did the professor do?

Hint on page 243.
Answer on page 291.

26 When in Rome

Was the previous problem too easy? If so, try to come up with a way of proving that one-half of nine equals four.

Hint on page 244.
Answer on page 291.

27 Number Path

Place the numbers 1 through 20 in the grid on the next page so that they form a continuous chain. In other words, starting with 1, you must be able to get to 2 by going left, right, up, or down—but never diagonally—and so on, all the way to 20. Just make sure that the positions of 2, 7, 10, and 17 are just as you see them. There is only one solution. Can you find it?

Hint on page 244.
Answer on page 292.

	7	10		
	2			17

28 Seeing Is Believing?

If you continued drawing the line at the bottom left of the diagram on the next page, and kept going up, which line would you meet up with, A or B?

Hint on page 244.
Answer on page 292.

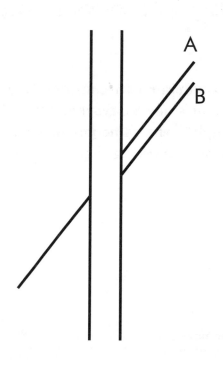

29 Two Workers Are Better Than One

If one worker can complete a job in 6 days and a second worker takes 12 days to complete the same job, how long will it take them working together?

Hint on page 244.
Answer on page 292.

30 An Odd Game of Bingo

Imagine playing a game of bingo using the card on page 57, on which all the numbers are odd!

The idea behind this particular game is that you must get a bingo—either across, up and down, or diagonally—that adds up to precisely 100. This can only be done in one way. Do you see how?

Hint on page 245.
Answer on page 294.

23	11	25	15	41
1	37	31	5	17
9	21	FREE	27	47
43	35	33	29	7
19	45	3	39	13

31 Diamond in the Rough

Of the four suits that make up a deck of cards, only the diamonds are symmetrical, in that a diamond—unlike a club, a heart, or a spade—looks the same whether it is rightside-up or upside-down.

However, one of the 13 diamond cards is different when you turn it upside-down. Without checking any decks of cards you may have lying around, can you name that one non-symmetrical diamond?

Hint on page 245.
Answer on page 294.

Three's a Charm

There is an inexpensive item that can be purchased for less than a U.S. dollar. You could buy it with four standard U.S. coins. If you wanted to buy two of these items, you'd need at least six coins. However, if you bought three, you'd only need two coins. How much does the item cost?

Recall that you have only five U.S. coins to work with: A penny (one cent), a nickel (five cents), a dime (ten cents), a

Hint on page 246.
Answer on page 294.

quarter (twenty-five cents), and a half-dollar (fifty cents).

33 Who Is the Liar?

Four friends—Andrew, Barbara, Cindy, and Daniel—were shown a number. Here's what they had to say about that number:

Andrew: It has two digits

Barbara: It goes evenly into 150

Cindy: It is not 150

Daniel: It is divisible by 25

It turns out that one (and only one) of the four friends is lying. Which one is it?

Hint on page 246.
Answer on page 295.

In the year 2000, April 1 (called April Fool's Day in many parts of the world) took place on a Saturday. On what day was April 1, 1999? What about April 1, 2001?

Hint on page 247.
Answer on page 296.

35 The Price of Fun

A Frisbee and a softball together cost $6.20. The Frisbee costs $1.20 more than the softball. How much does the Frisbee cost?

Hint on page 247.
Answer on page 297.

36 Fare Wars

Suppose a taxicab in Megalopolis charges 75 cents for the first quarter-mile and 15 cents for each additional quarter-mile. In Cloud City, a taxi charges $1.00 for the first quarter-mile and 10 cents for each additional quarter-mile.

What distance would produce the same fare for the two taxicabs?

Hint on page 247.
Answer on page 297.

37 The Powers of Four

Bert and Ernie take turns multiplying numbers. First Bert chooses the number 4. Ernie multiplies it by 4 to get 16. Bert multiplies that by 4 to get 64. Ernie multiplies that by 4 to get 256.

After going back and forth several times, one of them comes up with the number 1,048,576. Who came up with that number, Bert or Ernie?

Don't worry—the problem is easier than

Hint on page 248.
Answer on page 297.

it looks at first glance. You don't have to multiply the whole thing out to figure out the correct answer!

38 Square Dance

First count up the number of squares in the figure on page 73. Can you remove just four line segments to cut the total number of squares in half?

Don't leave any segments "hanging." Every segment must be part of at least one square.

Hint on page 248.
Answer on page 298.

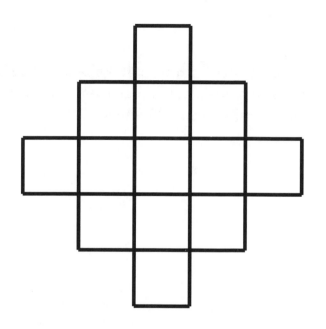

39 High-Speed Copying

If 4 copiers can process 400 sheets of paper in 4 hours, how long does it take 8 copiers to process 800 sheets?

Hint on page 248.
Answer on page 298.

COPYMATIC

40 **Divide and Conquer**

Fill in the boxes below to make the division problem work out.

```
        5 □
      ┌──────
  9 │ 4 □ □
    - □ □
      ──────
        3 □
      - □ □
        ──────
          0
```

Hint on page 248.
Answer on page 298.

Fill in the missing squares in such a way that the rows, columns, and the two diagonals all add up to the same number.

32	19		8
10	25		
9			
35	16		11

Hint on page 249.
Answer on page 299.

42 Comic Relief

While traveling in Russia, I bought six comic books for a total of seventeen rubles. Some of the comics cost one ruble, others cost two rubles, while the most expensive ones sold for ten rubles apiece.

How many of each type did I buy?

Hint on page 249.
Answer on page 299.

76

Please Fence Me In

Suppose you had a long stretch of fencing with which to make a nice big playpen for your new puppy Sam. If you wanted to give Sam the biggest possible area to roam around in, what shape should the fence be?

Hint on page 249.
Answer on page 299.

44 Prime Time

A number is called "prime" if its only factors are itself and 1. (Although 1 is not considered a prime number.) The first ten prime numbers are hidden in the square on the next page. Can you find them?

We suggest taking a pencil and filling in every square that contains a prime number.

Hint on page 250.
Answer on page 300.

32	16	24	33	45	28	54
40	23	2	11	5	19	12
14	36	10	55	17	34	49
6	50	38	13	22	51	20
21	35	3	46	27	18	39
9	29	48	15	4	52	26
55	44	25	8	42	30	1

A Pane in the Neck

The window in Harvey's living room has gotten very dirty. He asks a window washer how long the job will take, and the window washer says that it takes him 30 seconds to clean each 6 × 10 region. Harvey thinks that's a strange answer, until he realizes that 6 × 10 is the size of an individual pane. Well, how long will the entire job take?

Hint on page 250.
Answer on page 300.

46 Putting Your Two Cents In

Many years ago, when things cost a whole lot less than they do today, two brothers—Aaron and Bobby—went to the corner drugstore to purchase a pad of paper. Unfortunately, neither brother had much money. Aaron realized that he was two cents short of the price of the pad, while Bobby was 24 cents short. When they put their money together, they found that they still didn't have enough to purchase the pad!

How much does the pad cost?

Hint on page 250.
Answer on page 301.

47 Pieces of Eight

An octagon is an eight-sided figure. A stop sign is perhaps the most familiar example of a "regular" octagon, in which all eight sides have the same length. Inside the regular octagon on the next page, we have drawn three "diagonals"—lines connecting two of the extreme points. How many diagonals are there in all?

Hint on page 250.
Answer on page 301.

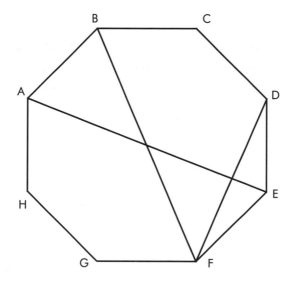

48 On the Trail

One of the numbers below becomes a common English word when converted into Roman numerals. Which one?

38   54   626

1,009   2,376   3,128

Hint on page 251.
Answer on page 302.

49 Spreading the Word

Suppose you want to make copies of pages 12, 19, 30, 31, and 47 of your pocket dictionary. If it costs a dime to make one copy, how many dimes will you need?

Hint on page 251.
Answer on page 302.

50 Surf's Up

At a surf shop in Malibu, California, a used blue surfboard is on sale for 100 dollars. According to the salesperson, the new price represents a 20% discount from the original price. What did it sell for originally?

Hint on page 251.
Answer on page 302.

91

51 The Big Inning of the End

On Sunday, May 7, 2000, the Houston Astros defeated the Los Angeles Dodgers 14-8, in ten innings. Where was the game played—in Houston or in L.A.?

Hint on page 251.
Answer on page 303.

Imagine that the diagram to the right represents city blocks. The idea is to walk from point S to point F, and of course you can only walk along the lines. The entire trip is five blocks long. In how many different ways can you make the trip?

Hint on page 252.
Answer on page 303.

S

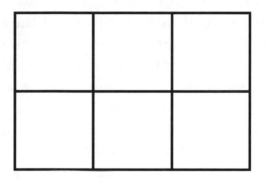

F

53 Apple Picking

Seventh Heaven Orchards decides to hold a special sale at the end of the season, hoping that people will come and buy the apples that have already fallen from the trees! They decide on an unusual system for pricing the apples. The bags they give out hold just seven apples each. The orchard then charges its customers five cents for every bag of seven apples, and 15 cents for every apple left over!

Hint on page 252.
Answer on page 304.

According to this system, which costs the most: 10 apples, 30 apples, or 50 apples?

54 Playing the Triangle

The triangle in the diagram has the lengths of two sides labeled. The reason the third side isn't labeled is that the labeler couldn't remember whether that side was 5 units long, 11 units long, or 21 units long. Can you figure out which it is? (Sorry, but the diagram is not drawn to scale!)

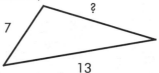

Hint on page 252.
Answer on page 305.

How Big?

In the figure below, we have drawn lines from each corner of a square to the midpoint of one of the opposite sides. How big is the smaller square in the middle —as compared to the original square?

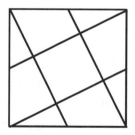

Hint on page 253.
Answer on page 306.

56 The Birthday Surprise

A math professor was lecturing his students on a remarkable fact in the world of probabilities. The professor noted that there were 23 students in the class, which meant that the likelihood that some two people in the room shared a birthday was 50 percent!

The professor expected the students to be surprised—most people figure that you'd need many more people before you'd have a 50% chance of a shared

Hint on page 253.
Answer on page 306.

birthday. Yet the class wasn't surprised at all. In fact, one student claimed that the professor had miscalculated, and that the likelihood of a shared birthday in the room was in fact much greater than 50%.

What had the professor overlooked?

57   Not Just Any Word Will Do

Little Ashley was trying to remember her father's phone number at the office: 269-1000. He explained to her that you could spell the word "any" by using letters that correspond to the 2, 6, and 9 on the dial.

But Ashley wanted a better word than ANY, so she stared at the dial. She eventually found five other words that could be formed using the letters from 269. Can you find those five words?

Hint on page 253.
Answer on page 307.

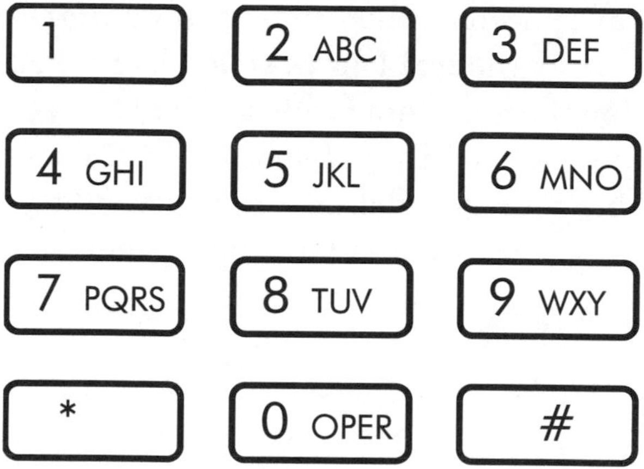
1
2 ABC
3 DEF
4 GHI
5 JKL
6 MNO
7 PQRS
8 TUV
9 WXY
*
0 OPER
#

Generation Gap

Grandpa Jones has four grandchildren. Each grandchild is precisely one year older than the next oldest one. One year Jones noticed that if you added the ages of his four grandchildren, you would get his age. How old is Grandpa Jones?

    A) 76

    B) 78

    C) 80

Hint on page 253.
Answer on page 307.

59 | The Run-Off

In a 10-kilometer race, Alex beat Burt by
20 meters and Carl by 40 meters. If Burt
and Carl were to run a 10-K race, and
Burt were to give Carl a 20-meter head
start, who would probably win?

Hint on page 254.
Answer on page 308.

60 The French Connection

Jason and Sandy took five tests during their first year in French class. Jason's scores were 72, 85, 76, 81, and 91. Sandy's scores were 94, 79, 84, 75, and 88. How much higher was Sandy's average score than Jason's average score?

Hint on page 254.
Answer on page 308.

Below is the digital display of a clock reading four minutes after four. As you can see, the hour and minute figures are the same. It takes one hour and one minute before you see this pattern again—at 5:05.

What is the shortest possible time between two different readings of this same type?

$$\boxed{4\!:\!04}$$

Hint on page 254.
Answer on page 309.

Staying in Shape

The figure below shows one way to join four squares at the edges and make a solid shape. How many different shapes can be created out of four squares? (Two shapes are not considered different if one can simply be rotated to produce the other.)

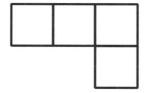

Hint on page 255.
Answer on page 309.

63 One of a Kind

To write out the number "fifteen," you need seven letters. When you write out "ten," three letters are required. There is one and only one number for which the number of letters needed is the same as the number itself! Can you find that number?

Hint on page 255.
Answer on page 310.

64 The Long Road

If you perform all the operations that are indicated, and end up with the number 97 in the circle, what number did you start with?

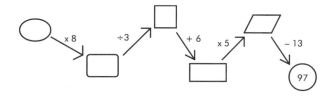

Hint on page 255.
Answer on page 310.

65 Whose Side Are You On?

Jeanne and Cindy play two sets in tennis. Jeanne starts on the sunny side (top) and Cindy starts on the shady side (bottom). According to the rules of the game, players switch sides after every odd game in each set. Assuming that Jeanne won the match, 6-3, 6-4, which side were the players on when the final point was played?

Hint on page 255.
Answer on page 310.

JEANNE

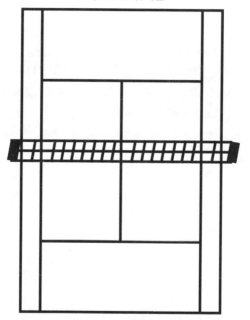

CINDY

66 If the Shoe Fits

A town has 20,000 people living in it. Five percent of them are one-legged, and half of the rest go barefoot. How many shoes are worn by the people in the town?

Hint on page 256.
Answer on page 310.

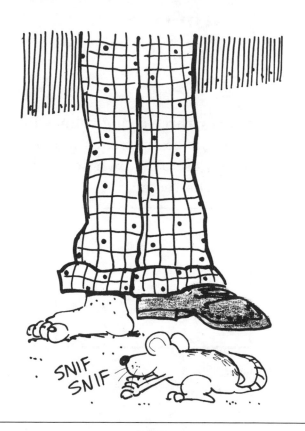

SNIF
SNIF

67 Win One For The Dipper

Can you draw three straight lines in the diagram below so that each star of the Big Dipper lies in its own separate region within the rectangle?

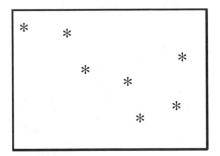

Hint on page 256.
Answer on page 311.

68 It All Adds Up

The sum of the digits of a certain three-digit number is 12. If the hundreds digit is three times the tens digit, and the tens digit is one-half the ones digit, what is the number?

Hint on page 257.
Answer on page 311.

We Can Work It Out

The dot-filled diagram is from an exercise bicycle at the health club. The numbers on the left stand for the degree of difficulty of the exercise. The higher the number, the greater the resistance offered by the bike, which increases the workout. The columns represents time: Each column stands for 5, 10, or 15 seconds, depending on the total time chosen.

Hint on page 257.
Answer on page 311.

But we don't have to worry about all that, because our task is a mental challenge, not a physical one. How many dots are there in all?

One last piece of advice: Don't count the dots one by one, or you'll go dizzy. There's a better way!

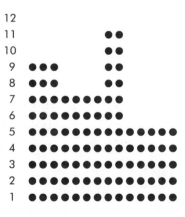

70 Going Crackers

A cracker company isn't pleased when it finds out the results of a survey it has taken. According to the survey, although customers would rather have a cracker than have nothing at all, those same customers would prefer peanuts to anything else!

A junior employee at the company decides that this is his big chance for a promotion. He claims to his boss that what the survey really said was that cus-

Hint on page 257.
Answer on page 312.

tomers prefer crackers to peanuts. How in the world could he come to that conclusion?

71 Don't Sneeze, Please

If the doctor says to take an allergy pill every three hours, how much time will go by between the first pill and the fourth pill?

...THIS PILL IS NOTHING TO SNEEZE AT!

Hint on page 257.
Answer on page 312.

72 Five Easy Pieces

In the diagram below, the big square is divided into four equal parts. Can you divide a square into five equal parts?

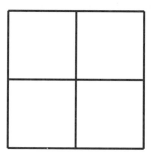

Hint on page 258.
Answer on page 312.

73 It's in the Bag

One bag contains three red marbles and two blue marbles. A second bag contains two red marbles and one blue marble. If you could pick only one marble from one of the bags, which one would you choose if you wanted to give yourself the best possible chance to pick a red marble?

Hint on page 258.
Answer on page 313.

(74) Switching Sides

Start with nine dots arranged in a square. The diagram to the right shows how to join some of the dots to form a figure with five sides. What is the greatest number of sides that a figure formed in this way can have? Remember, the figure must be closed—no loose edges permitted.

Hint on page 258.
Answer on page 313.

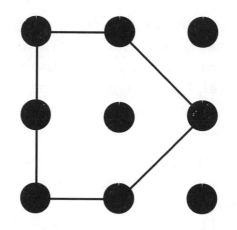

75 The Missing Shekel

A farmer in ancient Transylvania took his rutabagas to market each week. His standard price was three rutabagas for a shekel. On an average week, he sold 30 rutabagas and came home with 10 shekels.

One week, he agreed to sell the rutabagas grown by his neighbor, who wasn't feeling well enough to make the trip into town. The only surprise was that the neighbor's preferred price was two

Hint on page 259.
Answer on page 314.

130

rutabagas for a shekel. When the neighbor sold 30 rutabagas, he came home with 15 shekels.

The farmer decided that the only fair thing to do was to sell the combined crop at the rate of five rutabagas for two shekels. But when he added up his money after selling both his crop and his neighbor's crop, he had only 24 shekels, not the 25 he was expecting.

What happened to the missing shekel?

Using six 1's and three plus signs, can you form an expression that equals 24?

Hint on page 259.
Answer on page 314.

Thick As a Brick

If the diagram shows one face of a chimney, how many bricks are required to build the entire chimney? Remember, no bricks are cut in half.

Hint on page 259.
Answer on page 314.

What Do They Play?

Stacy, Alex, and Meredith play golf, chess, and soccer, but not necessarily in that order. Can you use the following clues to figure out which plays which?

A: Stacy gave the soccer player a ride to the last game.
B: The chess player said that Stacy drives too fast.
C: Meredith went to the prom with the chess player's brother.

Hint on page 259.
Answer on page 315.

In the diagram on the next page, nine playing cards are set up to form a rectangle. Assuming that the area of the rectangle is 180 square inches, what is its perimeter? (The perimeter is the distance around the entire rectangle.)

Hint on page 260.
Answer on page 316.

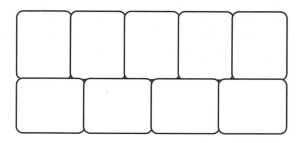

80 Class Dismissed

Suppose school starts promptly at 9:00 A.M. If each period lasts 40 minutes and there are 5 minutes between periods, when will the fourth period end?

Hint on page 260.
Answer on page 316.

81 Quarter Horses

Two horses live on a large piece of land shaped like a quarter-circle. The horses' owner wants to give each horse its separate space by building a fence on the property, but it is important that the two horses have the same space in which to run around. On the next page are three ways in which a straight fence can be installed to divide the area precisely in two. Which fence is the shortest? Which is the longest?

Hint on page 260.
Answer on page 317.

A   B

C

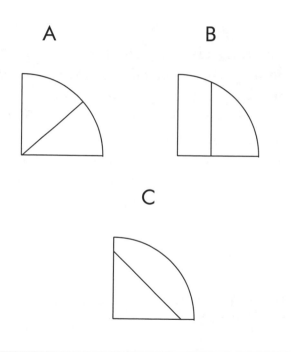

Begin by crossing out the letter N. Now go around the circle, counter-clockwise, crossing out *every other* letter you come across. If you keep going in the fashion, what will be the last letter? Remember, once you have crossed out a letter, you do not count that letter as you go around the circle a second or third time.

Hint on page 261.
Answer on page 317.

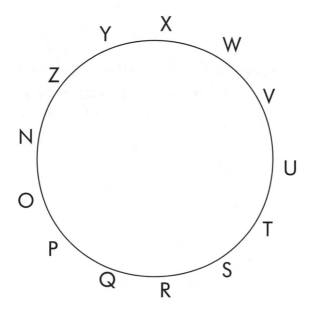

83 Once in a Century

In Eleventown, the citizens hold a big parade on January 1st of every year that is divisible by the number 11.

Well, a funny thing happened during the 1900s. As you recall, the nineteen hundreds were divided into ten decades, as follows:

The aughts: 1900–1909
The teens: 1910–1919
The twenties: 1920–1929

Hint on page 261.
Answer on page 318.

The thirties: 1930–1939
The forties: 1940–1949
The fifties: 1950–1959
The sixties: 1960–1969
The seventies: 1970–1979
The eighties: 1980–1989
The nineties: 1990–1999

In one and only one of these decades, there is no number divisible by 11. In which decade was there no parade in Eleventown?

84 The Conversion Machine

If you give the conversion machine a number, it will put the number through three separate steps. First of all, the machine will divide the number by 5. Then it will multiply the new number by 9. Finally, the machine will subtract 32 from the result.

One of the following numbers *remains the same* after it has been put through all three stages of the conversion machine. Which one is it?

Hint on page 262.
Answer on page 319.

85 On All Fours

Using just basic addition, subtraction, multiplication, and division, can you form each of the numbers from 1 through 10 using precisely four 4's?

To give you an idea of how this works, we'll start you off:

$$1 = (4 + 4)/(4 + 4)$$

$$2 = (4 \times 4)/(4 + 4).$$

The rest is up to you!

Hint on page 262.
Answer on page 319.

86 The Easy Way Out

What is (138 × 109) + (164 × 138) + (138 × 227)? Can you do it without multiplying everything out?

Hint on page 262.
Answer on page 320.

87 Kangaroo Numbers

A kangaroo number is a number that shows one of its factors. For example, any number with a zero at the end is a kangaroo number—560 has 56 as a factor. (5 also divides evenly into 560, but to be a kangaroo number, the factor must be more than one digit long.) The digits also have to be in order. (In 560, 56 is a factor, but 65 is not.)

Now that you know how they work,

Hint on page 263.
Answer on page 320.

which of the following numbers are kangaroo numbers?

A) 125   B) 664

C) 729   D) 912

Blind Date

Choose a weekday between October 9 and October 20 in the calendar on the next page. Add to it all the numbers in the 3 × 3 square that surround it. Now divide this total by 9. What is your answer?

Hint on page 263.
Answer on page 320.

OCTOBER 2000

S	M	T	W	T	F	S
1	2	3	4	5	6	7
8	9	10	11	12	13	14
15	16	17	18	19	20	21
22	23	24	25	26	27	28
29	30	31				

Does Gold Glitter?

"All that glitters is not gold," the teacher said.

"You mean that gold isn't the only thing that glitters?" Tracy asked.

"No," Sean interrupted, before the teacher could answer. "He means that gold doesn't glitter."

Well, who's right?

Hint on page 263.
Answer on page 321.

90 A Game of Chicken

Chicken McNuggets come in packages of 6, 9, and 20. Suppose you wanted to purchase 99 McNuggets for you and your friends. Assuming you wanted to buy as few individual packages as possible, how many of each size would you order?

Hint on page 264.
Answer on page 320.

Divide the figure below into four identical pieces.

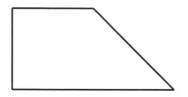

Hint on page 264.
Answer on page 322.

Hex-a-Gone

Drawing just three lines, can you transform the hexagon to a cube?

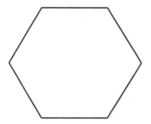

Hint on page 265.
Answer on page 322.

93 **Reel Life Story**

A group of seven adults went to the movies. The total cost of the movie tickets was $30.

This doesn't seem possible, does it? After all, 30 is not evenly divisible by 7. Ah, but there's a hitch. The reason that $30 *was* the total cost was that some members of the group were senior citizens, so they got to see the movie at half price.

Hint on page 265.
Answer on page 323.

How many of the group were senior citizens, and how much did the tickets cost?

94 Jack in the Box

Of six cards chosen from a full deck of playing cards, two are jacks. Suppose you placed all six cards in a box and selected two at random. Which is more likely— that you will select at least one jack or that you will select no jacks at all?

Hint on page 265.
Answer on page 323.

See You Later, Calculator

Which is bigger, 18 percent of 87, or 87 percent of 18? And don't multiply this out!

Hint on page 265.
Answer on page 324.

96

All in Black and White

Start with the number of seasons in a year. Multiply by the number of planets in the solar system. Add the number of cards in a complete deck—without the jokers.

What you end up with is another special number, but one that isn't quite as well known as the three numbers you've just seen. Do you know what makes the final number special?

Hint on page 266.
Answer on page 324.

Sweet Sixteen

Of the fifteen snowmen pictured here, no two are alike: Some have white eyes, others have black eyes; some are smiling, others are frowning; some have eyebrows, others do not; finally, some have noses, and others do not.

Because there are four different features, the total possible number of snowmen equals 2 × 2 × 2 × 2 = 16. Can you draw the missing snowman?

Hint on page 266.
Answer on page 325.

98 The Right Stuff

Ninety people applied for a job as a salesperson for a book publishing company. Ten of the applicants had never worked in sales or in the publishing business. Sixty-five had worked in sales at some point, and fifty-eight had some background in publishing.

How many of the applicants had experience in *both* sales and publishing?

Hint on page 266.
Answer on page 325.

At the top of page 171 is a "magic" triangle. What makes it magic is that the numbers on each of the three sides of the triangle add up to 12. Can you place the numbers from 1 through 6 in the blank triangle at the bottom in such a way that each of the three sides of the new triangle adds up to 10?

Hint on page 267.
Answer on page 326.

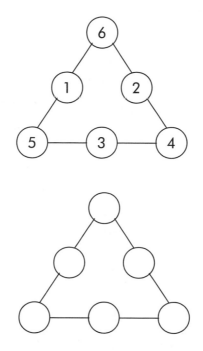

An Updated Classic

Sixteen matchsticks have been arranged to form a backward "L." See if you can add eight matches to form a region separated into four identical smaller regions. It's an old problem, but not everyone realizes that there are two completely different ways of solving it. Can you find one of these solutions?

Hint on page 267.
Answer on page 326.

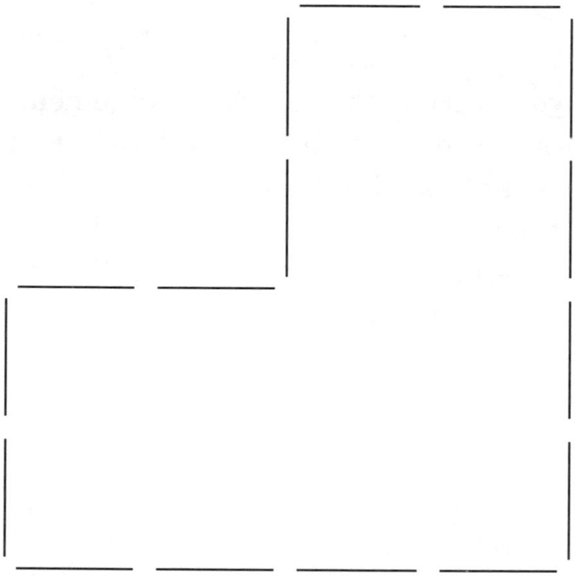

101 Eight Is Enough

If you start with a 3 × 3 arrangement of dots, there are 8 different-shaped triangles that can be drawn by connecting 3 of those dots. To get you started, two of those eight triangles have been drawn in on the next page. Can you find the other six?

Hint on page 267.
Answer on page 327.

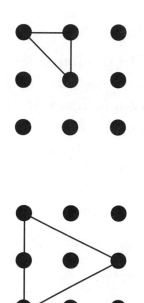

102 **Where's Waldo?**

Waldo is in the fourth grade. In Waldo's class, everyone sits in the same chair every day, and there are the same number of kids in every row. One day a substitute teacher came in and asked where Waldo was sitting. He was too shy to answer, so several of his classmates answered for him:

Maria said, "Waldo sits in the third row."

Hint on page 268.
Answer on page 327.

Jerry said, "Waldo sits in the fourth row from the back."

Alice said, "Waldo sits in the second seat from the right."

Oliver said, "Waldo sits in the fourth seat from the left."

How many students are in the class?

The Twelve Days of Christmas

The song "The Twelve Days of Christmas" includes some well-known presents:

A partridge in a pear tree
Two turtle doves
Three french hens
Four calling birds
Five gold rings
Six geese a-laying
Seven swans a-swimming
Eight maids a-milking

Hint on page 268.
Answer on page 328.

Nine drummers drumming
Ten pipers piping
Eleven dancers dancing
Twelve lords a-leaping

Throughout the entire song, including all
twelve "verses," which present shows up
most often? (For example, "two turtle
doves" counts as *two* presents every time
that phrase is sung.)

104   Oh, Brother!

Jeff was watching his older brother Matt do his math homework. Matt said that the assignment was about factorials, a subject much too complicated for Jeff to understand.

"What's the exclamation point?" Jeff asked, looking at the strange expression 8! in the middle of his brother's notes.

"It's a factorial symbol," Matt said.

"Well, what's a factorial?" Jeff asked.

Hint on page 268.
Answer on page 328.

Matt said, "A factorial is when you take all the whole numbers less than or equal to a particular number and multiply them all together. So 10! = 10 × 9 × 8 × 7 × 6 × 5 × 4 × 3 × 2 × 1. Now do you believe me when I say these things are hard?"

"I guess so," Jeff said. "But what's the problem you're working on?"

"I have to figure out what 8! divided by 6! is," Matt said.

Two seconds later, Jeff said, "I see the answer."

How did Jeff figure out what 8!/6! was without multiplying the whole thing out?

105 Numbers on the House

Suppose the town planning commission decides to buy brand-new house numbers for all of the residents of Sleepy Hollow Road. There are 50 houses on the road, numbered 1–50. How many of each number will they need?

Hint on page 269.
Answer on page 329.

106 Square Feet

A group of soldiers was marching in a square formation when 32 of them were called off for a training mission. The remaining soldiers regrouped and continued their marching, this time forming a smaller square. They continued to march until eight of them had to leave to run an obstacle course.

How many soldiers were there originally?

Hint on page 269.
Answer on page 329.

Incomplete Sentences

Place the appropriate sign—addition, subtraction, multiplication, or division—between the numbers 6, 3, and 2 to make the following number sentences true.

Hint on page 269.
Answer on page 330.

$$6 \quad 3 \quad 2 \quad = \quad 5$$

$$6 \quad 3 \quad 2 \quad = \quad 20$$

$$6 \quad 3 \quad 2 \quad = \quad 7$$

$$6 \quad 3 \quad 2 \quad = \quad 4$$

108 X Marks the Spot

Can you place five more X's in the grid so that every row and column has an even number of X's in it?

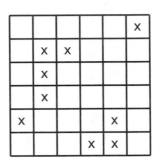

Hint on page 270.
Answer on page 330.

109 He Was Framed!

Jennifer bought a picture frame for a 4"
× 6" picture of her boyfriend. The outside of the frame measures 5" × 7". If the
picture fits inside perfectly, how wide is
the frame?

Hint on page 270.
Answer on page 331.

The Christmas Carolers

A group of Christmas carolers came across a neighborhood of five houses, as shown on page 191. It had just snowed, and the carolers wanted to create a path with their footsteps joining every pair of houses. They also wanted to visit every house on their journey. They didn't mind visiting a house more than once, but their rules didn't permit walking on a path they had already been on.

Hint on page 270
Answer on page 331.

Suppose they start caroling at the Andersons—house A. Where will their journey end?

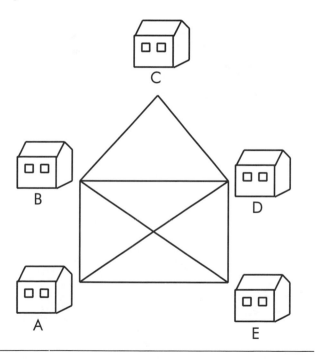

Forever Young

Heather was born in the winter of 1966. In April of 2006 she claimed to be only 39 years old. How can this be?

Hint on page 270.
Answer on page 332.

112 All in the Family

Each of the four Strickland brothers has a sister. Altogether, how many kids are in the family?

Hint on page 271.
Answer on page 332.

113 Squaring the Circle

In the diagram, a circle is nested inside a large square, then a smaller square is tilted and nested inside the circle. How big is the tilted square in relation to the larger one?

Hint on page 271.
Answer on page 333.

Too Close for Comfort

See if you can place the numbers 1 through 8 into the boxes below so that no two consecutive numbers are touching—either horizontally, vertically, or diagonally!

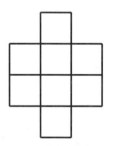

Hint on page 271.
Answer on page 333.

Stay Out of My Path!

The idea of this puzzle is to connect the four pairs of similar squares: the gray with the gray, the X mark with the X mark, and so on. But can you connect the four pairs so that none of the four pathways crosses any of the others?

Hint on page 272.
Answer on page 334.

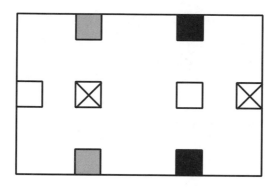

Hundred's Place

Suppose the "skyscraper" pattern to the right kept going and going. Would the number 100 belong to a short column, a medium column, or a tall column? Can you figure this out without writing out all the numbers in between?

Hint on page 272.
Answer on page 334.

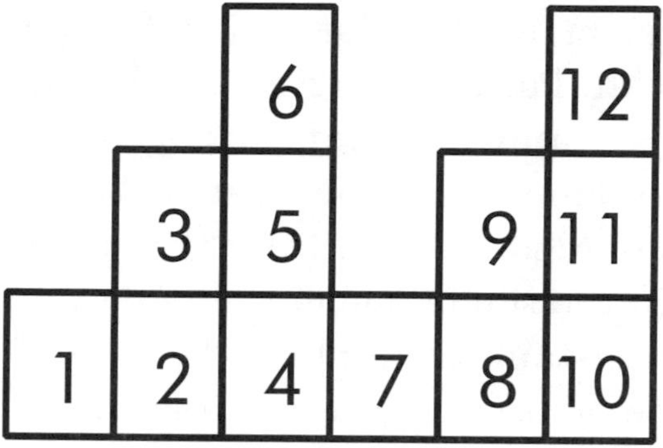
6
12
3
5
9
11
1
2
4
7
8
10

Occupational Hazards

Three men—Mr. Baker, Mr. Carpenter, and Mr. Potter—work as a baker, a carpenter, and a potter, but none of the three men has a job that matches his name. Also, each of the three men has hired the son of one of the other men as an assistant; again, though, none of the three sons works in a profession that matches his name.

If Mr. Carpenter is not a potter, what does young Mr. Baker do?

Hint on page 272.
Answer on page 335.

Straightening It Out

There are seven pieces, labeled A through G, in the crooked shape at the top of the next page.

There are eight pieces in rectangle at the bottom. One piece has been added from the crooked shape and another has been turned over. Can you identify these two pieces?

Hint on page 273.
Answer on page 335.

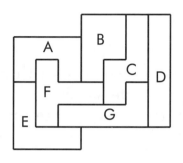

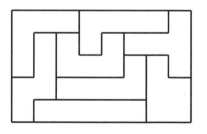

119 Misery Loves Company

Two investors—we'll call them Smith and Jones—made some unfortunate decisions in the stock market: Smith lost 60% of his money and Jones lost 85%. Jones was so discouraged he took his money out and put it into a savings bank. Smith, on the other hand, made some additional investments in an effort to get his money back. But he wasn't any luckier the second time around—he lost *another* 60%!

Hint on page 273.
Answer on page 336.

Well, neither of them made a very strong showing, that much is certain. But who did worse, Smith or Jones?

Melanie was given three positive numbers and told to add them up. Jessica was given the same three numbers and told to multiply them all together. Surprise, surprise: Melanie and Jessica got the same answer!

What numbers were they given?

Hint on page 273.
Answer on page 336.

The AMAZING STRANGE ...but TRUE!!!

121 **Number Ghost**

The idea behind the following puzzle is to start with the number 2681 and choose a number that begins with the same digit that 2681 ends with, which is 1. Once you find it you need to locate another number, one that starts with the same number that your new number ended with—kind of like a game of Ghost, but with numbers. Keep going in this way so that you form a chain of numbers. The chain stops when you find

Hint on page 274.
Answer on page 336.

a number whose last digit is 2—which happens to be the first digit of 2681. Can you make a chain that is longer than four numbers from among those below?

2681	1247	8499	5023	4387
5687	2309	7829	1235	6885
9123	6403	1569	4862	1298
5342	5706	8914	3190	6283

Double Trouble

It is possible to place the numbers 1 through 9 in the nine boxes below so that both of the multiplications in the sequence are correct. The numbers 3, 7, 8, and 9 have been placed for you. Can you figure out where the other five numbers go?

☐ 8 × 3 = ☐ 7 ☐ = ☐ 9 × ☐

Hint on page 274.
Answer on page 337.

123 Prime Territory

We know that a prime number is a number whose only factors are itself and 1. We also know that there is only one even prime number—and that is 2. Now for the puzzle, which is to find a three-digit number with the following properties:

A) Each of the three digits is a prime number, and

B) Each of those digits divides evenly into the three-digit number.

Hint on page 274.
Answer on page 337.

Say the Magic Words

Three favorite words of magicians are ABRACADABRA, PRESTO, AND SHAZAM! If each letter is given a value from its position in the alphabet (A = 1, B = 2, and so on), and you add up the values for each word, which would have the highest value?

Hint on page 275.
Answer on page 337.

125   **A Famous Triangle**

The diagram shows the first six rows of a famous mathematical construction called Pascal's Triangle. The way the triangle works is that 1's are placed on the outside edges, and each number on the inside is the sum of the two numbers above it. For example, the 6 in the middle of the fifth row is the sum of the two 3's from the fourth row.

Okay, now that you know what Pascal's

Hint on page 275.
Answer on page 338.

Triangle is, what is the sum of all the elements of the unseen *seventh* row?

Note: You don't have to figure out the numbers in the seventh row in order to figure out its sum!

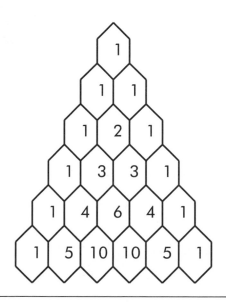

126

Last Train to Clarksville

Brian, Amy, and Stephanie are waiting at the train station. Each of the three is waiting for a different train. When they check the station clock, they realize that Amy is going to have to wait twice as long for her train as Brian will for his, while Stephanie will have to wait twice as long as Amy!

What time is it?

Hint on page 275.
Answer on page 339.

DESTINATION	TRACK	DEPARTURE
NEWBURGH	3	4:48
SPRINGFIELD	7	4:57
CLARKSVILLE	4	5:15

127

Follow the Directions

There are several different ways of putting the numbers 1 through 5 into the circles on the next page so that both directions—North-South and East-West—add up to the same number. But your question is a different one: Whatever way you happen to choose, the middle number will be the same. What is that number?

Hint on page 275.
Answer on page 339.

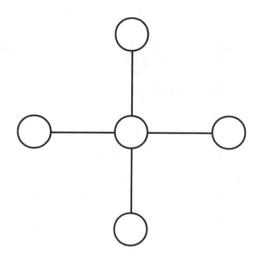

128 Crossing the Bridge

In the game of bridge, a standard deck of 52 playing cards is dealt among four people. The cards held by a particular player are called that player's "hand." Players assign a value to their hands by counting 4 points for an ace, 3 points for a king, 2 points for a queen, and 1 point for a jack. Sorry, but you don't get points for any other card.

Suppose that you are dealt a hand with one ace, three 7's, two 5's, and two 4's.

Hint on page 276.
Answer on page 340.

Even without looking at your other cards, what is the greatest number of points you could possibly have in your hand?

129 **Showing Your Age**

For their twentieth wedding anniversary, Richard and Sylvia had a party for several of their best friends. Things were going along just fine until one of their friends asked the happy couple who was older! Here's what they had to say.

Richard: "I am older than my wife."

Sylvia: "I am younger than my husband."

That might have been the end of it, but one of the guests knew that at least one

Hint on page 276.
Answer on page 340.

member of the couple was lying. Well, who is older, Richard or Sylvia?

130 Test Patterns

Can you locate a copy of the 3 × 3 square below in the 9 × 9 square on the next page?

Hint on page 276.
Answer on page 341.

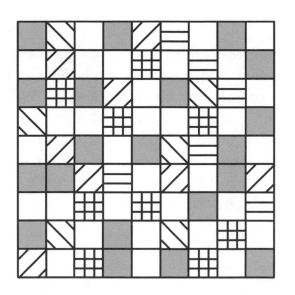

131   **Cookie Monster**

A bag contains three cookies, and each of them is different: one chocolate chip, one oatmeal raisin, and one sugar cookie. Elmo reaches in and picks one cookie, then Peter does the same. Who has the better chance of ending up with the sugar cookie—Elmo, who went first, or Peter, who went second?

Hint on page 277.
Answer on page 341.

132 Letter Logic

In the addition each letter stands for a number. Different letters must stand for different numbers, and if the same letter is repeated, it must stand for the same number each time. To give you a head start, one of the numbers has been revealed to be a 5.

$$
\begin{array}{r}
\text{END} \\
+\ \text{5G} \\
\hline
\text{GAME}
\end{array}
$$

Hint on page 277.
Answer on page 342.

1) What must the "G" stand for?
2) What must the "E" stand for?
3) Can you solve the entire puzzle?

... I LIKE TO DO THINGS BY THE *LETTER!!*

133 Miles to Go

The "odometer" of a car tells you how far it has traveled in its lifetime. The "trip odometer" can be reset at any time to tell you the length of a particular trip. Suppose the main odometer of a new car is at 467 and the trip odometer is at 22. How many miles do you have to travel before the main odometer is precisely two times the trip odometer?

Hint on page 278.
Answer on page 343.

The End Is in Sight

134

Starting with the "T" at the top of the diagram and moving from one diamond shape to another *touching* diamond shape, in how many ways can you spell out "THE END?"

Hint on page 278.
Answer on page 344.

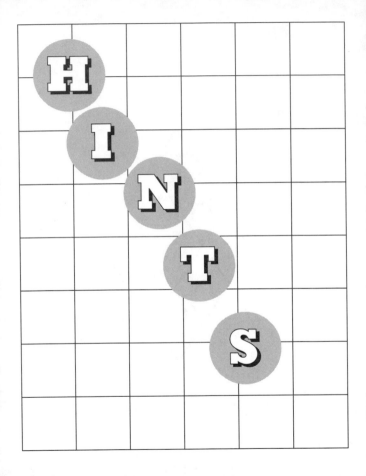

1   Easier by the Dozen

The puzzle would not be possible if the figures didn't overlap. Pay careful attention to the numbers that are multiples of 3— namely, 3, 6, 9, and 12.

2   Waiting in Line

Careful. The answer is not 14.

3   Magic Circle

First figure out the sum of all nine numbers. Divide that sum by 3, and you have the sum of each of the three smaller groups.

4   Who Is Faster?

How long does it take Hector to run the distance eight times?

⑤ Eggs-actly

When the problem asked you to be careful, that's a warning to watch out for a trick!

⑥ The Average Student

Knowing that the average of the ratings must be four, you start out with a three-point difference between the one-star rating (given to Melissa on her first assignment) and the desired four-star average. Well, how many stars can you make up at a time?!

⑦ Just Checking

Remember, if Ted plays against Jennifer, Jennifer is also playing against Ted! If you like, you can use A, B, C, D, and E for the kids, and then list all the one-on-one match-ups.

8 Big Difference

To find the biggest difference, try creating the biggest possible number.

9 Not Such a Big Difference

Find two numbers that are close together.

10 The One and Only

Trial and error will get you there! Note that the answer has more than one digit, which is sort of a clue right there. And you should be able to rule out two-digit numbers in bunches.

11 Letter Perfect

The new phrase also consists of three words, and one of them is left unchanged!

12 Countdown

Remember, a rectangle is any four-sided figure where the sides meet each other at 90 degrees—in other words, head on.

13 Short Division

The big number can be broken into many pieces, each of which is divisible by 7.

14 Square Route

All three lines go beyond the boundary of the square.

15 The Missing Six

More trial and error. If the "7" in the puzzle was replaced by a "6," no answer would be possible.

16 No Honor among Thieves

Assume first that the Scarecrow is guilty, then proceed to the other two suspects, one at a time. See if you come across anything that contradicts your assumption of guilt.

17 Circular Reasoning

In order for a line to divide the circle into two equal parts, that line must go through the center of the circle.

18 Trick or Treat

Remember, Mr. Greensleeve has fewer than 20 candies remaining, and many possibilities can be ruled out immediately. Try listing the numbers from 1 to 20 and crossing them out as you go along.

19 Donut Try This at Home

If a regular donut has, say, 100 calories, how many does a low-calorie donut have?

20 The Long Way Around

Do the "steps" in the figure really change anything? Remember, you *do* have enough information to solve the problem. We guarantee it!

21 Connect the Dots

The answer is actually a very familiar shape. If you can figure this one out, you're a real star!

22 Pickup Sticks

Twenty-nine is an unusual number. No other number would work in its place in this problem. Note, for example, that it doesn't have an "o" in it!

23 Starting to Waffle

Translate the rate of the portable machine into waffles per second. That way you can compare the two rates directly.

24 A Very Good Year

The year could not be in the 2000s or the 2100s, because the middle number would start off *less* than the first two digits. So start with the year 2200 and work from there. You need to do a little trial and error—but not too much!

25 Long Division

Professor Mathman was being tricky. It's easier to do the problem if you think in terms of the number 8 rather than the word "eight."

26 When in Rome

Like problem #23, the answer to this one is visual in nature. Don't forget the title.

27 Number Path

You won't have much trouble figuring out where 8 and 9 go. From there it's on to 6, 5, and so on. Be careful not to back yourself into a corner.

28 Seeing Is Believing?

Try looking at the diagram at an angle.

29 Two Workers Are Better than One

One way to figure out the problem is to find

out what portion of the job does each worker accomplishes in one day. But if you don't want to work with fractions, just ask what the two workers would accomplish in 12 days—working together, of course.

30 An Odd Game of Bingo

Some of the rows are just too big to add to 100. But there's another clue: Is 100 odd or even? Is the sum of five odd numbers odd or even? You don't have to do much actual addition to solve this problem, because you can rule out many of the answers before you even begin!

31 Diamond in the Rough

The idea is to visualize how the diamonds are put on the cards. The only hint you'll need is that there are never three diamonds in a row *across* the card, although for the higher numbers there are certainly three or more diamonds in a row going *down* the card.

32 Three's a Charm

It's probably easiest to look at the combinations of two coins. What combinations of two coins produce a number that is divisible by 3? For example, a quarter plus a penny equals 26 cents, which is not divisible by 3, so this combination can be ruled out. On the other hand, a nickel plus a penny equals 6 cents, which is divisible by 3 but isn't nearly big enough to satisfy the problem! One you get the right combination of two coins, you can work backward to get the rest of the answer.

33 Who Is the Liar?

First assume that Andrew is lying, and see if it is possible for Barbara, Cindy, and Daniel to all be telling the truth. Then do the same for the other three. In only one case will there be only one liar.

34 No Foolin'

There are 365 days in most years, almost precisely 52 weeks. "Almost," that is. The fact that 365 is not evenly divisible by 7 is at the heart of the problem.

35 The Price of Fun

You don't need algebra to solve this puzzle, though it would help. A little trial and error should see you through, but you'd better make sure that the difference between the cost of the two items is $1.20.

36 Fare Wars

What is the initial cost difference between the two cabs? How does it change every quarter-mile?

37 The Powers of Four

If you kept multiplying by 4, that would lead you to the right answer, but an easier approach is to look for patterns.

38 Square Dance

Remember when you're counting up all the squares, you need to include squares of different sizes.

39 High-Speed Copying

Questions like this one have been around for a lot longer than there have been copiers! The best approach is to look at the number of copies an individual can make, and go on from there.

40 Divide and Conquer

Start by multiplying the 5 and the 9 to get

the second row of the division. That should get you rolling.

41 Agent 86

If you add up the numbers in the first column, you will find out the sum for every row, column, or diagonal. Then go on to those rows or columns containing three out of the four possible numbers, and you'll be able to figure out the fourth. Pretty soon you'll be all done!

42 Comic Relief

How many ten-ruble comic books can there be?

43 Please Fence Me In

All that you need for this one is common sense. You're not being asked to come up with proof that one shape is best. Now that would be tougher!

44 Prime Time

At first glance, there are only nine prime numbers in the diagram. But if you follow the directions carefully, you might find the tenth one.

45 A Pane in the Neck

Remember that when the window washer has finished the job, Harvey should be able to see out the window perfectly.

46 Putting Your Two Cents In

The fact that the pad doesn't cost much is important to the solution, because many people tend to overlook the actual solution.

47 Pieces of Eight

Be sure not to "double-count" the diagonals.

The diagonal joining A to E is the same as the diagonal joining E to A.

48 On the Trail

Remember that I = 1, V = 5, X = 10, L = 50, C = 100, D = 500, and M = 1,000.

49 Spreading the Word

Another trick question—will they never stop?! Just make sure to take a close look at the page numbers.

50 Surf's Up

A common guess is $120, but that's not right.

51 The Big Inning of the End

In baseball, the home team bats last.

52 From Start to Finish

Let A stand for across and D for down. How many different combinations can you make of 3 A's and 2 D's? (For example, AAADD corresponds to traveling from the Start to the Finish along the outermost route. There are many other routes.)

53 Apple Picking

There is nothing tricky about the calculations here, but the answer may be a surprise.

54 Playing the Triangle

It is not possible to take just any three numbers and form a triangle with those numbers as the lengths of the sides. Remember, the shortest path between two points is a straight line.

55 How Big?

Try putting together the shapes that surround the central square.

56 The Birthday Surprise

For this particular class, the likelihood of a shared birthday was almost 100%!

57 Not Just Any Word Will Do

Four of the words are familiar nouns, while the fifth word is an adjective that may not be quite as familiar.

58 Generation Gap

Trial and error may work out here. You might also save some time if you notice that one of the three ages has a property that the other two do not have.

59 The Run-Off

It's a trick question. The trick is to see that the race between Burt and Carl will not be a tie.

60 The French Connection

You can figure out the average grade for each student by adding up the individual test scores and dividing by five. But if you look closely at the test scores, you may find a shortcut.

61 Mirror Time

There are twelve such times during each twelve-hour span. Going from 1:01 to 2:02 takes one hour and one minute; same for going from 2:02 to 3:03. But there is one occasion when the time gets shorter.

62 Staying in Shape

Pencil and paper are really required for this one.

63 One of a Kind

Fortunately, the number you're looking for isn't all that big. But you suspected that, right?

64 The Long Road

This problem has to be done backwards. Work from right to left, and do the opposite of what you're told to do!

65 Whose Side Are You On?

For those of you who have never played tennis, all you need to know is that a typical tennis match is the best two-out-of-three sets, and to win a set you must be the first player to win six games. Some matches involve tiebreakers for close sets, but tiebreakers weren't necessary for this particular match. Remember, in this match Jeanne and Cindy would have switched sides after the first set.

66 If the Shoe Fits

Read the puzzle carefully. On the other hand, it might interest you to know that the number five—as in five percent—doesn't really have much to do with the solution.

67 Win One for the Dipper

Use a ruler and use pencil! Also, you might want to look at the page from an angle, just to make sure that you can draw a line through certain spaces.

68 It All Adds Up

The most a single digit can be is nine, so you don't have that many choices.

69 We Can Work It Out

The problem is best tackled by separating the dots into rectangles. Just figure out the number of dots in each rectangle, then add them up.

70 Going Crackers

The secret to this one is in the wording. You have to find something that is both "better" than peanuts and "worse" than crackers. Sometimes there's nothing tougher than a good logic problem!

71 Don't Sneeze, Please

Another trick question. Read it carefully, and

put yourself in the position of the person who is taking the pills—even if you don't have allergies!

72 Five Easy Pieces

Don't forget the title. Whatever you do, you don't want to make this one harder than it really is.

73 It's in the Bag

The idea is to calculate the two probabilities as fractions, then to compare those fractions.

74 Switching Sides

Trial and error is the best approach. Remember that you don't have to use each and every dot.

75 The Missing Shekel

Is the price of five rutabagas for two shekels as fair as it looks?

76 Store 24

All you have to do is put the 1's together in the right way.

77 Thick as a Brick

How many bricks are required to build a single row?

78 What Do They Play?

This problem is solved by ruling out rather than ruling in. And keep in mind that Meredith didn't go to the prom with her own brother!

79 House of Cards

Figure out the dimensions of each individual card.

80 Class Dismissed

Don't forget that the number of periods and the number of breaks between periods are not the same!

81 Quarter Horses

The simplest thing to do is to compare each length to the radius of the circle. The radius of the circle is the length of either of the straight lines that form the quarter-circle.

82 And Then There Was One

Just keep going, and don't forget that once a letter has been crossed out, it has disappeared for the purposes of this puzzle. And use pencil!

83 Once in a Century

One of the toughest problems in this book. The key fact is that if a set of ten consecutive numbers contains no multiple of 11, then the very next number must be a multiple of 11. So if a decade—which ends in a year ending in 9—does not contain a multiple of 11, then one of the numbers of the form 1910, 1920, 1930, etc. *is* divisible by 11. The answer is the decade that comes *before* this number!

84 The Conversion Machine

This one is pretty simple. Just follow the same rules as the machine, and you'll find the magic number.

85 On All Fours

It might help to know that you can create 0 with two 4's $(4 - 4)$ and 1 with two 4's $(4/4)$. These are useful building blocks in making the numbers $1 - 10$.

86 The Easy Way Out

Don't perform the indicated multiplications. Note that 138 is repeated in all three expressions. Even better, the other numbers add up to a nice round number.

87 Kangaroo Numbers

Remember that an even number cannot possibly divide evenly into an odd number. This will help you reduce the number of possibilities.

88 Blind Date

The hint is that you're looking right at the answer!

89 Does Gold Glitter?

There's no right or wrong here, but you are encouraged to try and see things from Sean's point of view.

90 A Game of Chicken

Try subtracting 6's and 9's from 99 until you get a multiple of 20.

91 Four of a Kind

If you divide the figure as shown below in the following way, you can see that the total area equals six small squares (five are intact, and the other two halves combine to make the sixth one). So if you want to divide this figure into four equal pieces, the size of each piece must be $6\frac{1}{4}4 = 1\frac{1}{1}42$ small squares. Go from there!

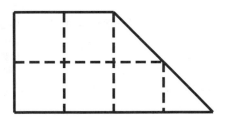

92 Hex-a-Gone

Try separating the hexagon into three diamond-shaped pieces and see what happens!

93 Reel Life Story

Trial and error will win the day. Note that the price of a senior ticket must divide evenly into 30.

94 Jack in the Box

Count out all the possibilities and see how many involve no jacks.

95 See You Later, Calculator!

Remember, you don't need to make any calculations to solve this one—or have you forgotten the title already? Common sense is the winner here.

96 All in Black and White

A deck of cards—without the jokers—contains four suits of 13 cards apiece, for a total of 52 cards. The rest is up to you!

97 Sweet Sixteen

Note that precisely eight of the sixteen total snowmen must have any one of the facial features described in the puzzle. So if you see that eight of the 15 original snowmen do not have eyebrows, the 16th *must* have eyebrows! And so on.

98 The Right Stuff

If you add up all the numbers, you'll get something way too big. But you're on the right track as long as you subtract the right number from your total.

99 Magic Triangle

The key to the puzzle is figuring out the corner numbers. In the example given, the sum of each leg was as big as possible (12), so you had to use the three biggest numbers in the corners, where they would count twice. To get 10, you have to make a change.

100 An Updated Classic

One of the solutions takes place totally inside the "L" shape, and the other one ventures outside.

101 Eight Is Enough

Make sure that you have exhausted all possibilities for the lengths of a side of a triangle that can be formed by the set of dots.

102 Where's Waldo?

Drawing a diagram is one way to get the solution. Don't forget that there is an equal number of students in each row—without that, you couldn't figure out the total number of students.

103 The Twelve Days of Christmas

Forget about the partridge. He appears the most often, but only comes one at a time!

104 Oh, Brother!

Don't worry about the exclamation point. You don't have to multiply out either 8! or 7!, but you *do* need to see that "cancellation" makes the problem easier.

105 Numbers on the House

Count them up by considering the tens place and the ones place individually. Then put the totals together.

106 Square Feet

The question is, what number is a perfect square and stays a perfect square when you subtract 32 from it? Don't worry, the number of soldiers is less than 100, so the number of soldiers on either side of the square is a single-digit number. But remember that the second square must have more than eight men in it.

107 Incomplete Sentences

Remember that you perform the various operations (addition, subtraction, multiplication, division) from left to right.

108 X Marks the Spot

By definition, each row and column must have either 2 or 4 X's in it.

109 He Was Framed!

This is a trick question. The answer is *not* one inch.

110 The Christmas Carolers

Just be careful and use a pencil. This puzzle is an example of an advanced mathematical principle, but you don't need to know the principle in order to solve the puzzle. Remember, you can (and must) visit some houses more than once.

111 Forever Young

Another trick question. We never said where Heather lives.

112 All in the Family

The puzzle states that each of the brothers has a sister. It doesn't say that each of the brothers has his *own* sister.

113 Squaring the Circle

Puzzles like these are often solved by drawing extra lines so that you can see the answer any calculations. Try drawing the two diagonals of the tilted square and see if that helps!

114 Too Close for Comfort

The two boxes in the middle hold the key to the solution. Since the idea of the puzzle is to keep close numbers far apart, you might want to start by making sure that the numbers in the two middle boxes are far apart!

115   Stay Out of My Path!

Two of the routes are fairly direct, but the other two are long and windy. Try to use space wisely. Don't crowd yourself out. It's okay for two paths to run alongside each other for a stretch, but they must not cross.

116   Hundred's Place

Note that the top number in each of the tall columns is a multiple of 6. If you use this pattern, you can see what happens around the number 100 without writing out all the numbers.

117   Occupational Hazards

You should be able to figure out Mr. Carpenter's job based on the information in the puzzle. Once you have his job, you can figure out his son's job, and so forth.

118 Straightening It Out

Looking at right-hand rectangle, each time you see a piece from the crooked shape, check off both pieces. That should lead you to the added piece.

119 Misery Loves Company

Suppose they each started out with one thousand dollars. After the first losses, Smith had $400 and Jones had $150. Now you have to work out how much Smith had left after his second 60% loss. (We are not including any interest that Jones might have earned from his savings account.)

120 Strange but True

Don't look too far. As a general rule, the bigger the numbers you choose, the greater the difference will be between their sum and their product. And if that's true for two numbers, it's certainly true for three!

121   Number Ghost

Remember that the chain must have at least five different numbers in it!

122   Double Trouble

You can figure out the ones digit of the three-digit number from the information you have already. Then try and figure out the missing number on the far left.

123   Prime Territory

The only single-digit numbers that are prime are 2, 3, 5, and 7. Is 5 in the number we're looking for. If so, in what position would it have to go?

124   Say the Magic Words

Just because a word is long that doesn't mean its "value" is high. Check out all the A's in ABRACADABRA!

125   A Famous Triangle

See if you can find a pattern in the sums of the first six rows.

126   Last Train to Clarksville

The first step is to figure out how much time goes by between the departures of the various trains. There is only one possibility for the current time.

127   Follow the Directions

You can solve the puzzle by trial and error, and the middle number of any solution is the middle number of *every* solution! But there's also a common sense approach that might give you the answer even without placing numbers in all five positions.

128 Crossing the Bridge

Remember, a deck of cards consists of four suits of 13 cards apiece. There are only four aces, and the same holds for kings, queens, and jacks.

129 Showing Your Age

See what happens if you assume that precisely one of the two—Richard or Sylvia— isn't telling the truth.

130 Test Patterns

Just try and focus on the diagram without going dizzy! One strategy is to look for a couple of particular squares in the smaller pattern, and see where they come up again within the larger pattern. In other words, don't try to memorize the entire 3 × 3 pattern!

131 Cookie Monster

As with many puzzles, you can solve this one by using numbers or common sense or both. What if there were a third person? What would that third person's chances be of ending up with the sugar cookie?

132 Letter Logic

To figure out G, remember that "END" and "5G" are fairly small relative to "GAME." Once you have G, you can figure out A and E using the same idea. And once you have G and E you automatically have D, and so on.

133   Miles to Go

What is the gap between the two odometers?

134   The End Is in Sight

Don't forget that "THE END" contains *two* E's! From there you should be able to count up all the possibilities.

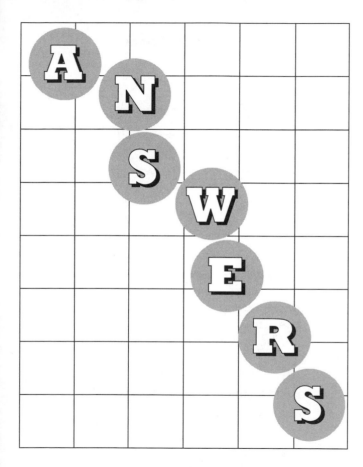

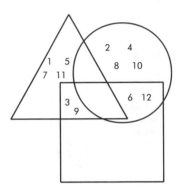

It's easy to guess 14, but the actual answer is 15 customers. To see why, suppose that only numbers 17, 18, and 19 were waiting. Now 19 -17 = 2, but clearly there are three customers, not two. The general rule is that you must subtract the two numbers and then add one.

③ Magic Circle

If you group the numbers as shown below,
you can see that the sum of the numbers in
each group equals 15. (4 + 5 + 6 = 15; 7 +
8 = 15; 9 + 1 + 2 + 3 = 15)

$$2 \quad ^{3}\!/\!_{4} \quad 5$$
$$1$$
$$^{9}\!/\!_{8} \quad 7 \diagdown^{6}$$

④ Who Is Faster?

Hector can run a mile in eight minutes, so
it takes him 64 minutes to run eight miles.
But Darius can run eight miles in just 60
minutes, so Darius is faster. There could be
another question here. Could Hector keep
up his eight-minute pace for an entire hour?
Maybe, maybe not. However, if he can't keep
it up, it proves that Darius is even faster!

5 Eggs-actly

Did you check the hint to see that it was a trick question? If the pot of water is big enough, four eggs can all be boiled at the same time, so it takes three and a half minutes to boil four eggs—same as with just one!

6 The Average Student

Three five-star homework papers will do the trick. Altogether they account for $3 \times 5 = 15$ stars. Adding the single star from the first homework gives 16 stars from four assignments, for an average of four stars per assignment.

Looking at the problem another way, note that the one-star homework paper was three stars under the desired average of four stars. Each five-star homework gains one point on the average, so it takes three of them to balance things out.

7 Just Checking

Each of the five kids plays four games, so it looks as though there must have been $5 \times 4 = 20$ games played in all. But wait! The game that Simon played against Theodore (for example) is the same game that Theodore played against Simon. You can't count the games twice. The actual number of games played equals $20/2 = 10$ games.

Looking at it another way, suppose the first player plays each of the others, for a total of 4 games. Then the second player plays the 3 remaining players (other than player #1), and so on. You get a total of $4 + 3 + 2 + 1 = 10$ games.

8 Big Difference

The biggest possible difference
is as follows:

$$
\begin{array}{r}
\boxed{7}\ \boxed{6} \\
-\ \boxed{2}\ \boxed{4} \\
\hline
5\quad 2
\end{array}
$$

9 Not Such a Big Difference

If we want the smallest possible difference instead, that
would be

$$
\begin{array}{r}
\boxed{7}\ \boxed{2} \\
-\ \boxed{6}\ \boxed{4} \\
\hline
8
\end{array}
$$

10 The One and Only

Forty is the number, as you can plainly see.
A B C D E **F** G H I J K L M N **O**
P Q **R** S **T** U V W **Y** Z

11 Letter Perfect

ELEVEN PLUS TWO can be rearranged to spell TWELVE PLUS ONE!

12 Countdown

There are 9 rectangles altogether: four small ones (A, B, C, and D), four that you get by putting the smaller ones together (A-B, A-C, B-D, and C-D), and of course the big one, A-B-C-D.

A	B
C	D

13 Short Division

$$\begin{array}{r} 71{,}091{,}051 \\ 7\overline{)\,497{,}637{,}357} \end{array}$$

The number 497,637,357 can be broken up into six pieces—49-7-63-7-35-7—each of which is divisible by 7. If you divide the five pieces one by one and then put them together, you get the answer shown above.

14 Square Route

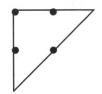

15 The Missing Six

There is more than one answer to this puzzle.

$$\boxed{2} + \boxed{5} = \boxed{7}$$

$$\boxed{4} - \boxed{3} = \boxed{1}$$

Here is another:

$$\boxed{2} + \boxed{5} = \boxed{7}$$

$$\boxed{4} - \boxed{3} = \boxed{1}$$

16 No Honor among Thieves

None of the three visitors is guilty.

If the Scarecrow were guilty, then his statement that the Tin Man was innocent would be false, so the Tin Man would also be guilty, but that cannot be the case. Similarly, the Tin Man can't be guilty, because otherwise the Cowardly Lion would also be guilty. And since the Tin Man must be innocent, his statement about the Cowardly Lion being innocent must be true. Therefore none of the three is guilty, just as it should be!

17 Circular Reasoning

Line C divides the circle into two equal pieces. It is the only line that goes through the center of the circle.

18 Trick or Treat

Mr. Greensleeve had 13 candies remaining. Note that whether you divide 13 by 2, 3, or by 4, you always get a remainder of 1. It is the only number less than 20 for which that is true.

19 Donut Try This at Home

Suppose a regular donut has 100 calories. If a low-calorie donut has 95 percent fewer calories, it must have 5 calories. Therefore you must eat 20 low-calorie donuts to get as many calories as you get from one regular donut.

20 The Long Way Around

The total distance around the diagram is 8 + 15 + 8 + 15 = 46 units. It makes no difference that the upper right portion of the diagram includes a set of "steps." That's because if you pushed out those steps, you could create an 8-by-15 rectangle, and the distance around that rectangle (its "perimeter") would be precisely 46 units.

21 Connect the Dots

A five-pointed star does the trick.

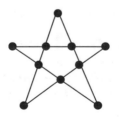

22 Pickup Sticks

$$TWENTY\ NINE = 29$$

23 Starting to Waffle

The stationary machine makes 3 waffles per second. If you had 4 stationary machines, you'd be making 12 waffles per second. The portable machine makes 120 waffles per minute, which is the same as 2 per second. To produce 12 waffles per second you would need 12/2 = 6 portable machines.

24 A Very Good Year

The next year to have the same property will be 2307: 23 + 07 = 30.

25 Long Division

Cover up the left half of the figure 8 below. What's left looks a lot like a 3, doesn't it?

8

26 When In Rome

Now cover up the bottom half of the figure below, which happens to be 9, in Roman numerals. What's left should give you 4, also in Roman numerals.

27 Number Path

6	7	10	11	12
5	8	9	14	13
4	1	20	15	16
3	2	19	18	17

28 Seeing Is Believing?

This problem is a bit of an optical illusion. The answer is line A, even though line B, at first glance, appears to be correct.

29 Two Workers Are Better than One

One way to solve the problem is to use fractions. The first worker completes the job in six days, so in one day he will have completed 1/6 of the total. Meanwhile, the second worker would complete 1/12 of the job in one day. Working together, they would complete 1/6 + 1/12 of the job in one day. 1/6 is the same as 2/12, so 2/12 + 1/12 = 3/12, which is the amount of the job they would finish in one day. 3/12 equals 1/4. So together they would complete 1/4 of the job in one day—therefore, it will take them 4 days to get the whole job done!

If you don't want to use fractions, you can do it another way. In twelve days, the first worker would complete the entire job twice, while the second worker would complete it once. Therefore, working together, they would complete three jobs in twelve days, which is a rate of one complete job every four days (12/3 = 4).

30 An Odd Game of Bingo

23	11	25	15	41
1	37	31	5	17
9	21	FREE	27	47
43	35	33	29	7
19	45	3	39	13

31 Diamond in the Rough

The only diamond that is not symmetrical is the seven of diamonds.

32 Three's a Charm

The item costs 17 cents. To purchase it requires four coins: one dime, one nickel, and two pennies. To purchase two items (34 cents) requires six coins: one quarter, one nickel, and four pennies. To purchase three items (51 cents) requires only two coins: one half-dollar and one penny.

33 Who Is the Liar?

Daniel is the liar. To see why, we examine one case at a time, using the fact that only one person is lying.

If Andrew were lying, the number would have three digits. (It couldn't have just one digit, because then it couldn't be divisible by 25, and Daniel would also be lying.) But if the number had three digits, either Barbara or Cindy would have to be lying, because 150 is the only three-digit number that goes evenly into 150. Therefore Andrew must be telling the truth, because there can only be one liar.

If Barbara were lying, then the number does not go into 150. But then either Andrew or Daniel must be lying, because the only two-digit numbers that are divisible by 25 (25, 50, and 75) all go evenly into 150. So Barbara must be telling the truth.

If Cindy were lying, then the number

would be 150. But then Andrew would also have to be lying, because 150 has three digits, not two. And we know Andrew is telling the truth.

So, the only possibility left is that Daniel is the liar, and this works out. If the number were 10, for example, Daniel would be lying, but the other three statements would all be true.

34 No Foolin'

April 1, 2001 is a Sunday. That's because one year is 365 days, or 52 weeks and one day. Any date moves ahead one day from year to year.

However, in a leap year, any date after February 29 moves ahead *two* days. The year 2000 was a leap year, so April 1, 1999 must have been a Thursday.

35   The Price of Fun

The Frisbee costs $3.70 and the softball costs $2.50. As you can see, the Frisbee costs $1.20 more than the softball, and together they cost $6.20.

36   Fare Wars

The distance that would produce the same fare on both meters is one and a half miles. That's because the Cloud City taxi starts out more expensive by 25 cents. Every quarter-mile, the Megalopolis taxi "makes up" five cents, so everything is even after five quarter-miles. But you can't forget the first quarter-mile, which makes six quarter-miles altogether. That's one and a half miles.

37   The Powers of Four

Ernie came up with the number 1,048,576. Note that all of Bert's numbers end in 4, while all of Ernie's numbers end in 6. That's all you need to know!

38 Square Dance

By taking out the four segments in the middle of the diagram, you reduce the number of squares from eighteen to nine (eight small squares and one big one).

39 High-Speed Copying

Eight copiers can process 800 sheets in 4 hours. Doubling the number of copiers will double the output without changing the amount of time required.

40 Divide and Conquer

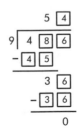

41 Agent 86

32	19	27	8
10	25	17	34
9	26	18	33
35	16	24	11

42 Comic Relief

One 10-ruble book, two 2-ruble books, and three 1-ruble books add up to six books and 17 rubles.

43 Please Fence Me In

If you make the pen in the shape of a circle, you will get the biggest area for a given amount of fencing.

44 Prime Time

The only one of the first ten primes that is left out of the original diagram is the number 7. But, as you can see, it makes an appearance if you shade in all the other primes.

32	16	24	33	45	28	54
40	23	2	11	5	19	12
14	36	10	55	17	34	49
6	50	38	13	22	51	20
21	35	3	46	27	18	39
9	29	48	15	4	52	26
55	44	25	8	42	30	1

45 A Pane in the Neck

There are 15 panes, each 6 × 10, and it takes 30 seconds to wash a 6 × 10 area, but remember that the windows must be washed on both sides! That means it takes one minute per pane, for a total of 15 minutes.

Why didn't Harvey just do it himself and spare everyone the trouble?

46 Putting Your Two Cents In

The pad costs 25 cents. Aaron had 23 cents and Bobby had one cent. Together they had 24 cents, which was a penny short.

47 Pieces of Eight

Each point from A to H (the "vertices" of the octagon) can be connected with five other points to form a diagonal. That seems to make a total of 8 × 5, or 40 diagonals. However, as it said in the hint, the diagonal from A to E is the same as the diagonal from E to A, and you can't double-count. You need to divide 40 by 2 to get the actual answer— 20 diagonals.

48 On the Trail

1,009 in Roman numerals is MIX. It is the only number that is a common English word in Roman numerals.

49 Spreading the Word

Four dimes are enough. Pages 30 and 31 are on the same spread, and because it is a pocket dictionary and therefore a small size, they could easily be copied on the same sheet

50 Surf's Up

The original price of the surfboard was $125. Twenty percent is one-fifth, and one-fifth of 125 is 25. If you subtract $25 from $125, you get $100, which is the sale price of the surfboard.

51 The Big Inning of the End

The game was played in Los Angeles. The key is that the most runs a team can score at any given moment is four—a grand slam. If the game had been played in Houston, it would have been over as soon as Houston, the home team, got the lead in the tenth inning. In other words, it is impossible for the home team to win by more than four runs in an extra inning game.

52 From Start to Finish

The total number of trips from S (Start) to F (Finish) equals 10. The easiest way to solve the problem is to use the diagram and count them up!

For a more systematic way to arrive at the answer, we start by observing that at each point you have a choice between moving across or moving down. Altogether you have to move across three times and down twice in order to get from S to F. So a pattern that would get you from S to F might look something like AADAD, where A means across and D means down.

Using our notation of A's and D's, the ten patterns are as follows:

AAADD	ADAAD
AADAD	DDAAA
AADDA	DADAA
ADDAA	DAAAD
ADADA	DAADA

53 Apple Picking

They all cost the same!

Ten apples = 1 bag (5¢) plus 3 apples at 15¢ each (45¢) = 50¢

Thirty apples = 4 bags (20¢) plus 2 apples at 15¢ each (30¢) = 50¢

Fifty apples = 7 bags (35¢) plus 1 apple at 15¢ (15¢) = 50¢

54 Playing the Triangle

The key to this puzzle is that if you add up the lengths of any two sides of any triangle, the sum must be greater than the third side. Why is this true? Because the shortest distance between any two points is a straight line. For example, in the diagram below, AB + BC could never be less than AC, because then the indirect route from A to C—stopping off at B along the way—would be shorter than the direct route!

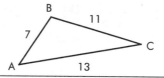

What this means is that 5 cannot be the third side, because $5 + 7 < 13$. In the same way, 21 is impossible, because $7 + 13 < 21$. That leaves 11 as the only possible answer.

55 How Big?

Note that the big square is divided into nine pieces: one square, four small triangles, and four odd-shaped four-sided figures (called trapezoids). Each of the four small triangles, when put together with one of the trapezoids, forms a triangle whose two pieces can easily be rearranged to form a square with the same area as the central square. Since there are a total of five identical squares, the central square is therefore one-fifth the area of the larger one.

56 The Birthday Surprise

The professor had forgotten that the class

included a pair of identical twins! (This is apparently a true story, the professor in question being famed logician and author Raymond Smullyan.)

57 Not Just Any Word Will Do

The five other words are bow, box, boy, cow, and coy.

58 Generation Gap

Grandpa Jones is 78. His four grandchildren are 18, 19, 20, and 21. Note that 18 + 19 + 20 + 21 = 78.

It is not possible for the sum of four consecutive numbers to be equal to 76 or 80. In general, the sum of four consecutive numbers will never be divisible by 4! (Both 76 and 80 *are* divisible by 4.)

59 The Run-Off

Burt will win. Why? Because when the two
of them ran against Alex, Burt was exactly
20 meters ahead of Carl at the moment Alex
crossed the finish line. Therefore, if Burt
were to give Carl a 20-meter head start, they
will be even at that point. But that point is
20 meters from the finish line, and Burt is
the faster runner. Therefore he would win
the race—but not by much!

60 The French Connection

One way to compute the average test scores
for the two students is to add up their individual test scores and divide by 5.

Average for Sandy = (94+79+84+75+88)/5
= 420/5 = 84

Average for Jason = (72+85+76+81+91)/5
= 405/5 = 81

Sandy has a three point advantage.

An easier way might be to arrange the test scores in the following way:

Sandy: 94 88 84 79 75

Jason: 91 85 81 76 72

It is now easy to see that Sandy has a three-point advantage the whole way through, so her average must be three points higher.

61 Mirror Time

The answer is 49 minutes, the time between 12:12 and 1:01.

62 Staying in Shape

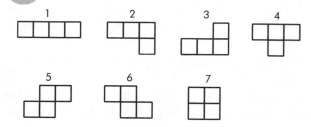

63 One of a Kind

The number is four.

64 The Long Road

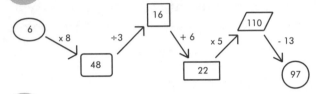

65 Whose Side Are You On?

Altogether there are 10 changes of sides, five per set—after the 1st, 3rd, 5th, 7th, and 9th games. Because 10 is an even number, the two players must have ended up on the same sides at which they began the match.

66 If the Shoe Fits

The total number of shoes is 20,000, the same as the total population of the town.

That's because the one-legged people wear one shoe, and, of the remaining people, half wear two shoes and half wear no shoes at all, for an average of one shoe per person.

67 Win One for the Dipper

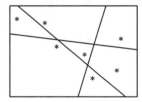

68 It All Adds Up

The number is 624.

69 We Can Work It Out

The total number of dots equals 102. The easiest way is to separate the dots into four rectangles: 3 × 9, 4 × 7, 2 × 11, and 5 × 5. That gives 27 + 28 + 22 + 25 = 102 dots.

70 Going Crackers

The junior employee argued that what the survey said was 1) Crackers are better than nothing, and 2) Nothing is better than peanuts. Putting the two together, you get that crackers are better than peanuts!

71 Don't Sneeze, Please

Nine hours. The time between the first pill and the fourth pill equals three intervals of three hours each.

72 Five Easy Pieces

It's a trick question, of course. A square can be divided into any number of equal parts simply by drawing vertical lines!

Pick the second bag. The second bag gives you a 2/3 chance of picking a red marble, while the chance of a red marble from the first bag is only 3/5. (To see that 2/3 is greater than 3/5, find the common denominator of 15: 2/3 = 10/15, while 3/5 = 9/15.)

The most number of sides you can have is 7. The diagram shows two ways of reaching this total. (There are many other solutions, some of which are simply rotations of the solutions above. Others involve sides consisting of more than one segment—for example, if you pushed out either lower diagonal of the right-hand figure, you would get a seven-sided figure with a squared-off corner.)

75 The Missing Shekel

The problem with the price of five rutabagas for two shekels is that the five rutabagas consist of 3 cheap ones (the three for a shekel variety) and 2 expensive ones (the neighbor's two for a shekel batch). By selling all 30 rutabagas in this manner, the farmer is basically selling 20 at his price and 10 at his neighbor's more expensive price—not 15 at each price. That's why he ends up a shekel short.

76 Store 24

$11 + 11 + 1 + 1 = 24$

77 Thick as a Brick

Here's what the first row of the chimney looks like from above. There are six bricks in this row. Because the chimney consists of five rows, there must be 5 × 6 = 30 bricks altogether.

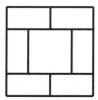

78 What Do They Play?

A: Stacy gave the soccer player a ride to the last game.
B: The chess player said that Stacy drives too fast.
C: Meredith went to the prom with the chess player's brother.

A) means that Stacy isn't the soccer player. B) means that Stacy isn't the chess player. Therefore Stacy plays golf. C) means that Meredith isn't the chess player, so she must be the soccer player. That leaves Alex as the chess player.

79 House of Cards

There are nine cards with a total area of 180, so each one must have an area of 20. The measurements of each card are therefore 4 × 5 (note that 4 × 5 = 20, and that the length of four cards in the diagram is precisely equal to the width of five cards). But if each card is 4 × 5, the height of the figure is nine inches and the length is 20 inches, so the perimeter equals 2 × (20 + 9) = 58 inches.

80 Class Dismissed

The fourth period will end at 11:55, or five minutes before noon. That's because the four class periods take up 4 × 40 = 160 minutes, while there are a total of 15 minutes between periods. That's 175 minutes in all, which is just five minutes less than 180 minutes, which is three hours.

81 Quarter Horses

B is shortest, A is in the middle, and C is longest. Note that A is just the radius of the circle, while B is clearly shorter than the radius. As for C, you can see from the picture below that the fence is longer than the radius. So, if C is longer than A, and B is shorter than A, you have your answer: B is the shortest and C is the longest.

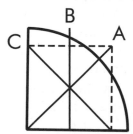

82 And Then There Was One

The only letter left standing is the letter W.

There was no parade during the 1970s. The key is to notice that because 11 is just one more than 10, the only way that a sequence of ten numbers can not contain a multiple of eleven is if the very next number *is* divisible by 11. (This fact was mentioned in the hint for this puzzle.)

With that in mind, one of the numbers 1910, 1920, 1930, etc. must be divisible by 11. The zero doesn't affect anything here, so what we really have is that one of the numbers 191, 192, 193, etc. is divisible by 11. We can see that 198 is the number we're looking for, because $198 = 11 \times 18$. (Simply add the digits 1 and 8 and put the result in the middle, and you have 11×18!!) But if 11 divides evenly into 1980, it also divides evenly into 1969 (180 − 11), but it does not divide evenly into any number in between, which takes care of 1970 through 1979, otherwise known as the seventies!

84 The Conversion Machine

The only number to stay the number after being put through the conversion machine is the number 40. You can see that 40/5 = 8, 8 × 9 = 72, and 72 − 32 = 40.

In real life, the conversion machine is similar to the transformation between two different temperature scales—the Fahrenheit scale and the Celsius, or Centigrade scale. The difference is that the only temperature to be the same in the Fahrenheit and Celsius scales is 40 degrees *below* zero—when we're too cold to care!

85 On All Fours

1 = (4 + 4)/(4 + 4)   3 = (4 + 4 + 4)/4
2 = (4 × 4)/(4 + 4)   4 = 4 + (4 − 4)/4

$5 = (4 \times 4 + 4)/4$ $8 = 4 + 4 + 4 - 4$

$6 = 4 + (4 + 4)/4$ $9 = 4 + 4 + 4/4$

$7 = 44/4 - 4$ $10 = (44 - 4)/4$

86 The Easy Way Out

$(138 \times 109) + (164 \times 138) + (138 \times 227) =$
$138 \times (109 + 164 + 227) = 138 \times 500 = 138 \times$
$1000/2 = 138,000/2 = 69,000.$

87 Kangaroo Numbers

The kangaroo numbers on the list are 125
and 912. Note that $125 = 25 \times 5$, while $912 =$
12×76.

88 Blind Date

The answer is your original number. The reason is that the middle number is the *average* of the eight numbers surrounding it—and therefore remains the average of all nine numbers in the 3 × 3 square. If you add up all the numbers surrounding and including 10, for example, you'll get 10 × 9. And dividing by 9 gives you 10, the number you started with.

89 Does Gold Glitter?

Tracy is probably right, because the expression "All that glitters is not gold" is supposed to mean that gold isn't the only thing that glitters. However, Sean has a good point. What he noticed was that if "all that glitters" means "everything that glitters," then it looks as though everything that glitters is not gold, which makes it look like there are many things that glitter, but that gold doesn't happen to be one of them!

It's probably best to stick with Tracy's version and not lose sleep over this one!

90 A Game of Chicken

Two packages of 6, three packages of 9, and three packages of 20 give you $(2 \times 6) + (3 \times 9) + (3 \times 20) = 12 + 27 + 60 = 99$ McNuggets.

91 Four of a Kind

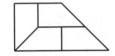

92 Hex-a-Gone

To create a cube, separate the figure into three diamond-shaped pieces. To see the cube, just tilt your head!

93 Reel Life Story

There were four senior citizens in the group. They paid $3.00 apiece. The other three adults paid the full price of $6.00 per ticket, for a total of $30.00 for the seven tickets.

94 Jack in the Box

Suppose you number the cards 1–6, with the jacks being numbers 1 and 2. There are 15 different ways of selecting two cards, as follows:

$$1-2 \quad 2-3 \quad 3-4 \quad 4-5 \quad 5-6$$
$$1-3 \quad 2-4 \quad 3-5 \quad 4-6$$
$$1-4 \quad 2-5 \quad 3-6$$
$$1-5 \quad 2-6$$
$$1-6$$

Of these 15, only the last three columns don't contain a jack. There are 6 choices among these three columns, so the chance of not choosing either jack is 6/15, or 2/5.

The chance of choosing at least one jack is 3/5, so that is the more likely event.

95 See You Later, Calculator!

18 percent of 87 equals 87 percent of 18. Technically, 18 percent of 87 equals (18/100) × 87 and 87 percent of 18 equals (87/100) × 18, but you don't have to do any multiplication or division to see that these two expressions are equal, simply because they involve the exact same numbers!

96 All in Black and White

The number of seasons in a year = 4.

The number of planets in the solar system = 9.

The number of cards in a complete deck = 52.

4 × 9 + 52 = 88, which happens to be the number of keys on a piano.

97 Sweet Sixteen

Here is the missing snowman. He seems happy that you found him!

98 The Right Stuff

The answer is 43. Simply add up 10 + 65 + 58, getting a total of 133, then subtract 90 to get the answer. The reason this works is that when you add up 10, 65, and 58, you are "double-counting" the people with experience in both sales and publishing (the group you're interested in). So just subtract the original number of applicants (90) and you're left with the experienced people— single-counted, just the way you want!

99 Magic Triangle

Here is one solution. Other solutions may be obtained by rotating this one to change the positions of the numbers, but the position of the numbers in relation to one another doesn't change.

100 An Updated Classic

You can either add to the original diagram and create four squares, as in the left diagram, or you can separate the original shape into four identical, smaller shapes.

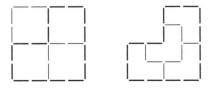

Eight Is Enough

Here are the eight patterns:

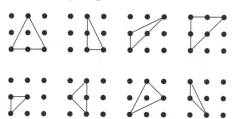

Where's Waldo?

Waldo's position must be as shown in the diagram. Because each row has the same number of students, they must fill up the entire 5 × 6 rectangle, for 30 students in all.

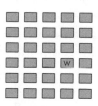

103 The Twelve Days of Christmas

The presents that show up the most are those of the sixth and seventh days—the geese a' laying and the swans a' swimming. The six geese are mentioned seven times, for a total of 42, and the seven swans show up six times, again for a total of 42. (The partridge shows up the most frequently, but only one at a time!)

104 Oh, Brother!

If you take the product of the first eight whole numbers—8 × 7 × 6 × 5 × 4 × 3 × 2 × 1—and divide by the product of the first six whole numbers—6 × 5 × 4 × 3 × 2 × 1—everything cancels out except the eight and the seven. That means $8!/6! = 8 \times 7 = 56$.

105 Numbers on the House

A total of 91 numbers are required—one each for the nine houses numbered 1–9, and two each for the houses numbered 10–50.

Of these 91, each of the numbers 1–4 is used 15 times, the number 5 is used 6 times, and each of the numbers 6–0 is used 5 times. Sure enough, $(4 \times 15) + 6 + (5 \times 5) = 60 + 6 + 25 = 91$.

106 Square Feet

There were 81 soldiers originally, marching in a 9×9 square. After 32 of them were called away, that left 49 soldiers, who then marched in a 7×7 square.

If not for the fact there are at least eight soldiers in the second square, there would have been a second solution: with 36 soldiers originally and 32 called away. Then you would have been left with 4, another perfect square!

107 Incomplete Sentences

$$\boxed{6} - \boxed{3} + \boxed{2} = 5$$

$$\boxed{6} \times \boxed{3} + \boxed{2} = 20$$

$$\boxed{6} + \boxed{3} - \boxed{2} = 7$$

$$\boxed{6} / \boxed{3} + \boxed{2} = 4$$

108 X Marks the Spot

The gray squares show two ways to add five new X's so that every row and column has an even number of X's.

109

He Was Framed!

As long as you didn't answer too fast, this one wasn't all that tough. The width of the picture frame was 1/2 of an inch. The trick is not to answer one inch—remember, the frame goes around all four sides of the picture!

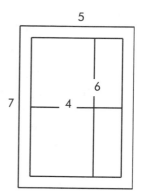

The Christmas Carolers

Believe it or not, the journey must end at house E. House E is the only other house with an *odd* number of paths leading from it. It is not possible to start at any house other than A or E and make a "closed loop" of the type the Christmas carolers set out to do.

111   Forever Young

The most likely explanation is that Heather was born in Australia, New Zealand or some other place in the Southern Hemisphere, where it is winter during the months that are summer for the Northern Hemisphere. That way she could have been born in, say, July, which means that she wouldn't have reached her 40th birthday as of April, 2006.

112   All in the Family

There are five kids in the family: four boys and one girl. Each of the brothers has a sister, all right—but it's the same one!

113   **Squaring the Circle**

When you join the diagonals of the tilted square, you divide the outside square into four smaller squares. But precisely one-half of each of these smaller squares is contained inside the tilted

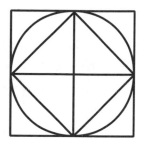

square, so the tilted square must be half the size of the outside square.

114   **Too Close for Comfort**

The figure at right is one solution. Another can be obtained by interchanging the two outer "columns." In either case, the middle boxes are occupied by the "1" and the "8."

	7	
3	1	4
5	8	6
	2	

115

Stay Out of My Path!

Here is one solution: Any other solutions use the same idea— you need to "wrap" two paths around one of the middle squares in order to keep from crossing lines.

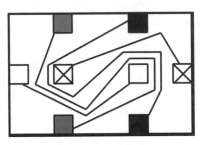

Hundred's Place

The number 100 is found at the base of a tall column.

Note that 96 is a multiple of 6, and all the multiples of 6 are located in the top spot of one of the tall columns. From there you just count a few more until getting to the magic 100.

117 Occupational Hazards

We know that Mr. Carpenter is not a potter (because the puzzle says so), and we also know that Mr. Carpenter cannot be a carpenter, because no one's job matches his name. Therefore Mr. Carpenter is a baker. We also know that Mr. Potter cannot be a potter, so Mr. Baker must be the potter, which leaves Mr. Potter as the carpenter.

As for young Mr. Baker, he is hired by one of the men other than his father. He cannot work for Mr. Carpenter, because he cannot be a baker. That means that he works for Mr. Potter; because Mr. Potter is a carpenter, young Mr. Baker must also be a carpenter!

118 Straightening It Out

There are two copies of piece G in the rectangle, and piece B must be turned over to make things work out.

119   Misery Loves Company

Jones did worse than Smith, even after Smith's second 60% loss. To see why, assume that each man started with $1,000, as suggested in the hint. Then Jones ended up with $150, following his 85% loss. Smith had $400 after his first loss. After his second loss he had $400 − (60% of $400). But 60% of $400 equals $240, so he ended up with $400 − $240 = $160, barely better than Jones. The key is that Smith's second 60% loss was made on a smaller investment—$400 versus $1,000.

120   Strange but True

The numbers are 1, 2, and 3. It's easy to check that $1 + 2 + 3 = 1 \times 2 \times 3 = 6$.

121   Number Ghost

The chain is 2681, 1235, 5706, 6885, 5342.

122 Double Trouble

$$\boxed{5}\,\boxed{8} \times \boxed{3} = \boxed{1}\,\boxed{7}\,\boxed{4} = \boxed{2}\,\boxed{9} \times \boxed{6}$$

123 Prime Territory

The only number that satisfies both conditions is 735.

124 Say the Magic Words

The values of the magic words are as follows:

ABRACADABRA = 1 + 2 + 18 + 1 + 3 + 1 + 4 + 1 + 2 + 18 + 1 = 52

PRESTO = 16 + 18 + 5 + 19 + 20 + 15 = 93

SHAZAM = 19 + 8 + 1 + 26 + 1 + 13 = 68

As you can see, PRESTO has the highest value. And even though ABRACADABRA is the longest word by far, it has the lowest value.

A Famous Triangle

The sum of the elements of the seventh row equals 64. To get this total, you have two choices. One is to figure out the elements of the seventh row and add them all up. The other thing you can do is notice the pattern of the earlier rows. You can see that the pattern, starting with the second row, goes 2, 4, 8, 16, and so on—each new row doubles the result of the row before! Continuing all the way to the seventh row, we get the same answer: 64.

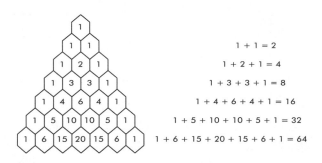

$$1 + 1 = 2$$
$$1 + 2 + 1 = 4$$
$$1 + 3 + 3 + 1 = 8$$
$$1 + 4 + 6 + 4 + 1 = 16$$
$$1 + 5 + 10 + 10 + 5 + 1 = 32$$
$$1 + 6 + 15 + 20 + 15 + 6 + 1 = 64$$

Last Train to Clarksville

It is now 4:39. Brian has to wait 9 minutes for his train (to Newburgh). Amy has to wait 18 minutes for her train (to Springfield), while Stephanie has to wait 36 minutes for her train (to Clarksville).

Follow the Directions

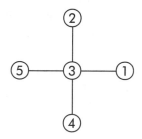

The middle number must be 3, which of course is also the middle number of 1, 2, 3, 4, and 5. The idea is that you can pair the 1 and 5 to give you a 6, and you can pair the 2 and 4 to give you another 6. But you can't pair the 3 with anything, which is why it has to go in the middle. The sum in any direction is 9. (There are four answers in all, obtained by switching the positions of the 5 and 1 or the 4 and 2.)

128 Crossing the Bridge

The one ace, three 7's, two 5's, and two 4's account for eight cards, so you only have five left (each hand has 13 cards). The greatest number of points you could have from those five cards would be 18—three aces (you already have one) and two kings. If you add those 18 points to the 4 points for the ace you already have, you would have a total of 22 points.

129 Showing Your Age

Richard and Sylvia's statements were consistent with one another, so either they were both telling the truth or both were lying. But if at least one of them was lying, then they both were. (We'll forgive them. It's their party, after all.) That means that Sylvia is older than Richard.

130 Test Patterns

The 3 × 3 square makes an appearance in the lower left section of the 9 × 9 square.

131 Cookie Monster

Elmo's and Peter's chances are both 11/43. Clearly this is true for Elmo, because when he chooses there are three cookies, only one of which is a sugar cookie. By the time Peter chooses his cookie, he will only have a chance at the sugar cookie in two out of three cases—when Elmo hasn't already picked it! But of those two occasions in three, Peter's chance at getting the sugar cookie will be 11/42, and 21/43 times 11/42 equals 11/43.

Another way to think of the puzzle is this: Suppose there was a third person—Max—who went *after* Elmo and Peter. Clearly Max will get the sugar cookie whenever it is the only one left, and the chances of that happening must be 11/43. But if Elmo's chances are 11/43 and Max's chances are 11/43, the same must be true for Peter—after all, someone must get the sugar cookie!

132 Letter Logic

G must stand for 1, because a three-digit number plus a two-digit number cannot be possibly be greater than 1,000. Similarly, the

E must stand for 9, because if it were anything less than 9, it couldn't carry over to
four digits after adding a two-digit number.
We also know that A must equal 0, for similar reasons. But we have D + 1 = 9, so D = 8.
The last step is the middle column, but the
only way to get a sum of 10 or greater (to
produce the carrying in the leftmost column)
without repeating letters is to have N = 7
and M = 2.

$$\begin{array}{r} 978 \\ + \ 51 \\ \hline 1029 \end{array}$$

 133 **Miles to Go**

The gap between the two odometers is 445
miles, a gap that will not change. Therefore,
the main odometer will be twice the trip
odometer when the trip odometer reads 445
miles. That will happen in precisely 445 –
22 = 423 miles.

The End Is in Sight

Suppose you start by moving to the H on the left. If you then move to the E on the left, you must then move to the E in the middle to begin the word END, at which point you have two choices for N. While if you move to the E in the center, you have two choices for the E that begins END, and only one choice for N. That's four paths if you start with the H on the left, and, using the same reasoning, you also get four paths if you start with the H on the right. Altogether, that's eight ways of saying THE END.

There is, actually, a ninth way of saying "The End," and you may like the ninth way better. Here goes:

Thanks for picking up a copy of *The Little Giant Book of Math Puzzles*. We hope you enjoyed it.

Puzzles by Level of Difficulty

The Toughest Puzzles

Index